FREDERICK WILLIAM MAITLAND

And the History of English Law

FREDERICK WILLIAM MAITLAND

FREDERICK WILLIAM MAITLAND AND THE HISTORY OF ENGLISH LAW

JAMES R. CAMERON

NORMAN
UNIVERSITY OF OKLAHOMA PRESS

The publication of this book has been aided by a grant from the
Ford Foundation

In honor of Bertha Haven Putnam (1872–1960)
an early disciple of
Frederick William Maitland's
who in her own books complemented
his great studies in the legal history
of Great Britain in the Middle Ages.

ACKNOWLEDGMENTS

WITHOUT ATTEMPTING TO NAME all of those to whom I am indebted for aid, I should mention particularly Warren O. Ault, now professor emeritus at Boston University, without whose inspiration, counsel, and encouragement I should never have completed this task. My wife, Ruth Allen Cameron, has rendered the many aids and services that only an author can fully appreciate. A word of appreciation should also be extended to the staffs of the libraries of Eastern Nazarene College, Boston University, and the Boston Public Library for their efficient and cheerful assistance.

James R. Cameron

Quincy, Massachusetts
January 20, 1961

CONTENTS

ILLUSTRATIONS

INTRODUCTION

FREDERICK WILLIAM MAITLAND HAS BEEN CALLED "The Historical Spirit Incarnate" by a former president of the American Historical Association.[1] Through the years he has acquired the reputation of being a "historian's historian," worthy to be ranked with Bishop Stubbs. This glib phrase can be thrown about with little understanding or real meaning when applied to a particular scholar. It may even mean that the scholar's writings are so abstruse that only a professional historian compelled by a sense of duty would ever turn to them. It is true that Maitland wrote little for the general reading public or, indeed, little that might be called general history. His subject, the history of English law, sounds formidable enough to discourage all but the hardiest or those who are specialists in the subject. But it is equally true that the writings of Maitland have been the starting point for many historians who wanted to explore subjects which he touched upon in his works.

In this process he has not escaped what seems to be a natural desire in man to knock down idols or images—the more re-

[1] Title of an article by Robert Livingston Schuyler, in the *American Historical Review* (hereafter *AHR*), Vol. LVII (1952), 303–22.

vered the image, the greater the satisfaction in destroying at least a portion of it. Just as William Stubbs was considered to represent the best in historical scholarship in his generation, so has Maitland been considered for his time. While many later scholars have turned to a statement by Maitland much as a minister taking a text for a sermon, others—and these seem more prevalent—have used such a statement for the purpose of destroying the image of him as the "historian's historian."[2] Often, however, historians have seized upon a suggestion or implication in his works and emphasized its novelty as the basis for a thesis they have expounded.[3]

Even the minor works of Maitland have been published to

[2] As I read through the volumes of the *English Historical Review* (hereafter *EHR*), I was particularly impressed by the number of articles which referred to Maitland; for example, Warren O. Ault, "Some Early Village By-Laws," Vol. XLV (1930), 208–31; C. R. Cheney, "Legislation of the Medieval English Church," Vol. L (1935), 193–224, 385–417; Mary Cheney, "The Compromise of Avranches of 1172 and the Spread of Canon Law in England," Vol. LVI (1941), 177–97; Barbara Dodwell, "East Anglian Commendation," Vol. LXIII (1948), 289–306; V. H. Galbraith, "The Making of Domesday Book," Vol. LVII (1942), 161–77; George L. Haskins, "The Petitions of Representatives in the Parliaments of Edward I," Vol. LIII (1938), 1–20; Robert S. Hoyt, "The Nature and Origins of the Ancient Demesne," Vol. LXV (1950), 145–74; Naomi Hurnard, "The Anglo-Norman Franchises," Vol. LXIV (1949), 289–320, 433–60; *ibid.*, The Jury of Presentment and the Assize of Clarendon," Vol. LVI (1941), 374–410; Elizabeth G. Kimball, "Tenure in Frank Almoign and Secular Services," Vol. XLIII (1928), 341–53; May McKisack, "Borough Representation in Richard II's Reign," Vol. XXXIX (1924), 511–25; Doris Rayner, "The Forms and Machinery of the 'Commune Petition' in the Fourteenth Century," Vol. LVI (1941), 198–233, 549–70; John Horace Round, "The 'Tertius Denarius' of the Borough," Vol. XXIV (1919), 62–64; Carl Stephenson, "Commendation and Related Problems in Domesday," Vol. LIX (1944), 289–310; *ibid.*, "The Anglo-Saxon Borough," Vol. XLV (1930), 177–207; *ibid.*, "The Aids of the English Boroughs," Vol. XXIV (1919), 457–75; James Tait, "The Firma Burgi and the Commune in England, 1066–1191," Vol. XLII (1927), 321–49; *ibid.*, "The Origin of Town-Councils in England," Vol. XLIV (1929), 177–202, 399.

[3] McIlwain, Pollard, Baldwin, and Richardson and Sayles.

make them more accessible to scholars.[4] These *Collected Papers* have long been out of print, and in recent years there have been published two selections of his writings that appear to have more lasting value.[5] This is only one indication of a revived interest in Maitland and his writings. He has also been the subject of a number of articles which have appeared in both historical and legal journals;[6] in addition, two collections of his letters have been published.[7]

An adequate but by no means definitive biography of Maitland was written soon after his death.[8] Although I have read all known published material on his life, this volume in no sense purports to be a biography. The significant facts are within easy reach of any who might seek them. I must comment, however, that Maitland's life is a stirring illustration of a man being driven to unusual heights of endeavor by a "thorn in the flesh." For nearly twenty years he lived in the

---

[4] *The Collected Papers of Frederick William Maitland*, ed. by H. A. L. Fisher (1911). Hereafter referred to as *Collected Papers*.

[5] *Maitland: Selected Essays*, ed. by H. D. Hazeltine, G. Lapsley, and P. H. Winfield (1937); *Selected Historical Essays of F. W. Maitland*, ed. by Helen M. Cam (1957). Hereafter referred to as *Selected Essays* and, *Historical Essays* respectively.

[6] R. J. White, "F. W. Maitland: 1850–1950," *The Cambridge Journal* (1950), 131–43; Mrs. Reynell, "A Memoir of F. W. Maitland," *Cambridge Law Journal*, Vol. XI (1951), 67–73; T. F. T. Plucknett, "F. W. Maitland," *New York University Law Review*, Vol. XXVI (1951), 1; *ibid.*, "Maitland's View of Law and History," *Law Quarterly Review* (hereafter *LQR*), Vol. LXVII (1951), 171–94; M. T. Rooney, "Maitland and the Corporate Revolution," *New York University Law Review*, Vol. XXVI (1951), 24; Schuyler, "The Historical Spirit Incarnate, Frederic William Maitland," *AHR*, Vol. LVII (1952), 303–22; H. Hollond, *Frederic William Maitland, 1850–1906: A Memorial Address* (1953); Ermengard Maitland, *F. W. Maitland: A Child's-Eye View* (1957).

[7] Warren O. Ault, "The Maitland-Bigelow Letters," *Boston University Law Review*, Vol. XXXVII (1957), 285–326; Austin Lane Poole, "Letters from Maitland to R. L. Poole, Editor of the *English Historical Review*," *Cambridge Historical Journal* (hereafter *CHJ*), Vol. X (1952), 318 ff.

[8] Herbert Albert Laurens Fisher, *Frederick William Maitland* (1910).

shadow of death and finally died while only in his middle years. The bibliography of his writings at the end of this book stands as a tribute to his amazing industry and achievement. There are two other bibliographies of Maitland's writings in print,[9] but I believe that mine is more complete and accurate than either of them.

Helen Cam has written a stimulating and provocative introduction to certain of Maitland's historical essays in which she suggests that recent scholars do not always agree with his conclusions. Although this work was begun before Miss Cam's book appeared, it has received inspiration from her approach.

Most, but by no means all, of Maitland's contributions to scholarship can be encompassed within the framework of the history of English law. I have selected the areas in which Maitland made his most notable contributions to our knowledge and understanding of the history of English law and have tried to explain the basis for his conclusions and to show where his contributions stand after more than half a century of historical research.

[9] *Frederic William Maitland: Two Lectures and a Bibliography*, ed. by A. L. Smith (1908); *The Frederic William Maitland Reader*, ed. by Vincent T. H. Delaney (1957).

FREDERICK WILLIAM MAITLAND

And the History of English Law

I

MAITLAND

AS A HISTORIAN

IT SEEMS ONLY APPROPRIATE that a study of Maitland's contributions to the history of English law should commence with a consideration of his concept of history. He came to history from the study of law, and the interrelationship of these two strains is evident throughout his writings. I do not mean to imply that Maitland was a narrow legal historian; this is far from the truth. Traditionally a lawyer is conservative in judgment and looks to the past only to find precedents for a case or evidence to sustain a preconceived opinion. Training in law normally does not result in historical-mindedness. Sir Frederick Pollock, who collaborated with Maitland in planning and writing *The History of English Law Before the Time of Edward I,* has described Maitland as "a man with a genius for history, who turned its light upon law because law, being his profession came naturally into the field."[1]

Maitland was certainly aware of the hazards of his profession, and he did not fall into the pattern of many lawyers who have written on history both before and since his time. He warns us that "we must not be in a hurry to get to the begin-

[1] "Frederick William Maitland," *LQR,* Vol. XXIII (1907), 401–19.

3

ning of the long history of law."[2] The historian of law, like any historian for that matter, must guard carefully against reading ideas of a later time into an earlier period and *vice versa*. Maitland warns us against the fallacy of believing that merely because our remote ancestors were simple folk they had simple law: "Simplicity is the outcome of technical subtlety; it is the goal not the starting point. As we go backwards the familiar outlines become blurred; the ideas become fluid, and instead of the simple we find the indefinite."[3] Extreme caution must be exercised in order to prevent reading our own ideas into the words used by our forebears. Medieval historians must be at least amateur etymologists. By way of example, Maitland tells us that "if we introduce the *persona ficta* too soon, we shall be doing worse than if we armed Hengest and Horsa with machine guns or pictured the Venerable Bede correcting proofs for the press."[4]

For Maitland the earliest English law could not be distinguished from custom. The conscious separation of law from morals and religion was a slow and gradual process. "The history of law must be a history of ideals."[5] The historian of law must strive to determine not only what men have said and done but what men have thought. In England this task gains significance from the fact that the connected and distinguishable legal life of the nation goes back to the time of Edward I. Undoubtedly this was an important factor not only in influencing Maitland to undertake his monumental work but also in defining the scope of the *History of English Law Before the Time of Edward I*. Although this work bears the joint author-

[2] *Domesday Book and Beyond*, 356.
[3] *Ibid.*, 9.
[4] *Ibid.*, 356.
[5] *History of English Law*, I, *xxiv,xxviii*; *Domesday Book and Beyond*, 356.

4

ship of Frederick William Maitland and Sir Frederick Pollock, Pollock wrote a preface in which he protested that although it had been jointly planned, Maitland had done by far the greater portion of both the actual research and the writing. Miss Cam tells us that Maitland wrote all of this work except the chapter on Anglo-Saxon law.[6]

Since Maitland was primarily a historian of English law, he recognized the importance of the divisions of labor in order that the advancement of knowledge might be facilitated. For him the history of law was an integral part of the history of England; indeed, "it was the key to the whole story."[7] He recognized that it was necessary to go outside of his own special field of interest in order to gain a complete understanding or explanation of the material under consideration. He readily acknowledged that the history of English towns "must not be merely the history of legal arrangements. The trade winds blow where they list, and defy the legislator."[8] Maitland undoubtedly gave more assistance to those laboring in neighboring vineyards than he received, by pointing out that "legal documents, documents of the most technical kind, are the best, often the only evidence that we have for social and economic history, for the history of morality, for the history of practical religion."[9] He certainly deserves some of the credit for the fact that medievalists today use legal documents as sources for social and economic history to a far greater extent than they did in the nineteenth century.[10]

Maitland's legal training caused him to be suspicious of gen-

[6] *History of English Law*, I, xxxiv, vi; *Historical Essays*, xiv.
[7] *Ibid.*, x.
[8] *Township and Borough*, 42.
[9] "Why the History of English Law Is Not Written," *Collected Papers*, I, 486.
[10] "Historical Spirit Incarnate," *AHR*, Vol. LVII (1952), 304.

eralizations. In instances in which generalizations were essential, he illustrated his general principles by applying them to specific cases. As Sir Paul Vinogradoff has suggested, "What he wanted most was to trace ideas to their embodiment in facts."[11] Maitland's ability to relate legal terms to personal experiences and meaningful patterns of thought is illustrated by his explanation of the meaning of the Anglo-Saxon term *sake:*

> It is still in use among us, for though we do not speak of a sake between two persons, we do speak of a man acting for another's sake, or for God's sake, or for the sake of money. In Latin therefore *sake* may be rendered by *placitum:* "Roger has sake over them" will become "Rogerius habet placita super eos"; Roger has the right to hold pleas over them. Thus easily enough *sake* becomes the right to have a court and do justice.[12]

It was Maitland's extensive knowledge of source material which enabled him to use this manner of exposition. He tried to use words to paint an image which would be correct and also intelligible to his readers. Although he preferred a concrete or case-related type of exposition, he was neither unable nor unwilling to resort to generalization when it was necessary or desirable. This becomes immediately apparent to anyone who reads his article on the Elizabethan settlement in the *Cambridge Modern History* or his article on the history of English law which appears in the *Encyclopaedia Britannica.*[13] Even in his more technical writings, however, "he exhibited

---

[11] "Frederick William Maitland," *EHR*, XXII (1907), 282.

[12] *Domesday Book and Beyond,* 84.

[13] "The Anglican Settlement and the Scottish Reformation," *Cambridge Modern History* (1934), II, 550–99 (reprinted in *Historical Essays*); "English Law," *Encyclopaedia Britannica* (1957), VIII, 564–69.

the rare combination of mastery of detail and high generalizing power."[14]

Maitland's concern for the history of English law was central to his whole professional career. Nearly everything that he wrote or edited was directly related to this general subject. Although he was probably not aware of it at the time, his inaugural lecture as Downing Professor of the Laws of England set the theme for his academic career. He tells us in the first place that the history of English law was not written because its study was isolated from every other study. Secondly, although English lawyers were exposed to a little knowledge of the history of English law, this was primarily medieval law as interpreted by modern courts to suit modern cases. This was hardly the historical method, nor did it lead to a very rapid increase in the knowledge of the history of law. Maitland pointed out that only a few of the men who chose the legal profession would succeed in it, and he suggested that some of those who failed would be admirably prepared to pursue the history of law.[15] This sounds like practical advice from one who knew whereof he spoke. Mr. Rogers, with whom Maitland read law for several years, wrote that although Maitland possessed "the clearest grasp of legal points and the utmost lucidity of expression, . . . I doubt if he would have succeeded as a barrister" because "he was the most retiring and diffident man that I ever knew."[16]

A Sunday afternoon stroll, on May 11, 1884, with the Russian scholar, Paul Vinogradoff, has been credited, by Maitland's biographer, with first calling to Maitland's attention the abundance of written records at the Public Record Office,

[14] Schuyler, "Historical Spirit Incarnate," *AHR*, Vol. LVII (1952), 310.
[15] "Why the History of English Law Is Not Written," *Collected Papers*, I, 487, 490, 496.
[16] Fisher, *Maitland*, 15–17.

from which the history of English law might be derived.[17] Several more recent writers have pointed out that Maitland had already been working in the Public Record Office before the supposedly climactic day described by Fisher.[18] Professor Plucknett has distorted Fisher's account to mean that Maitland's encounter with Vinogradoff was responsible for "Maitland's sudden conversion to legal history."[19] This interpretation can be readily disproved merely by referring to the Maitland bibliography at the end of this volume which indicates that Maitland's publications on legal history go back five years prior to this encounter. Actually Fisher merely stated that Maitland had told him personally of that Sunday talk:

> ... how from the lips of a foreigner he first received a full consciousness of that matchless collection of documents for the legal and social history of the middle ages, which England had continuously preserved and consistently neglected, of an unbroken stream of authentic testimony flowing for seven hundred years, of tons of plea-rolls from which it would be possible to restore an image of long-vanished life with a degree of fidelity which could never be won from chronicles and professed histories. His vivid mind was instantly made up; on the following day he returned to London, drove to the Record Office, and being a Gloucestershire man . . . asked for the earliest plea-roll of the county of Gloucester.[20]

[17] *Ibid.*, 24.

[18] As Miss Cam has noted in her introduction to *Historical Essays*, Maitland was at work in the Public Record Office in February of 1884. This statement is supported by F. M. Powicke, *Modern Historians and the Study of History*, 10, and Plucknett, "Maitland's View of Law and History," *LQR*, Vol. LXVII (1951), 85–87.

[19] "Maitland," *N. Y. U. Law Review*, Vol. XVI (1951); reprinted in *Maitland Reader*, 193–95.

[20] *Maitland*, 24 f.

We know that Maitland and Vinogradoff first met on a "Sunday tramp" arranged by Leslie Stephen on January 20 of the year in question. The facts would best be served if we assumed that it was on this first encounter that Vinogradoff shared the triumph of his discovery with his new-found friend. In recounting this event many years after it actually occurred, Maitland was probably confused in his own mind about the actual day. Undoubtedly the source of his knowledge was of far greater importance to Maitland than the exact day of the event. We have every reason to believe that Vinogradoff was the first to appreciate the value of the records stored in the Public Record Office. Maitland dedicated his first volume of legal records to him.[21] In a later letter to his friend, Maitland referred to this incident as "that day [which] determined the rest of my life."[22] One must conclude that it was Vinogradoff who first pointed out to Maitland the treasure in the Public Record Office. If this is so and Maitland was using the Record Office in February, then Vinogradoff must have confided in Maitland at their first meeting in January.

Maitland was also inspired by his grandfather, Samuel Roffey Maitland, and by his friend Frederick Pollock. In a letter to his sister, Maitland evaluated his grandfather's writings. It is of some interest to note that most of the things which he said about his grandfather's writings could be said with equal validity about his own.

> It is a book for the few, but then those few will be just the next generation of historians. It is a book which "renders impossible" a whole class of existing books. . . . One has still to do for legal history something of the work which Samuel Roffey

---

[21] *Pleas of the Crown for the County of Gloucester, 1221* (1884).
[22] Dated November 15, 1891.—Fisher, *Maitland,* 51.

Maitland did for ecclesiastical history . . . to teach men that some statement about the thirteenth century does not become the truer because it has been constantly repeated.[23]

Most of Maitland's writings revolve about the hub of English law. His earliest works were editions of legal records which he felt it was necessary to scrutinize in order to evaluate properly the workings of the early legal system.[24] The earliest court records which were available were those of the thirteenth century. He was forced, therefore, to begin at that point and to work in both directions. He first gave his attention to working backwards to the earlier period. In this, he followed the method of Frederick Seebohm.[25] It was necessary to spend much time analyzing the records of the Domesday survey. Although certain general results were incorporated in the *History of English Law,* Maitland found it necessary to extend his views in a separate and subsequent volume, *Domesday Book and Beyond.* He was aware of the danger his method entailed, but realizing that there was none other available, he proceeded with extreme caution to decipher this enigmatic period. If all of his conclusions have not stood up, they have at least provided a stimulus to other scholars.[26] The Ford Lectures for 1897 were a by-product of this research.[27] Maitland's monumental work ground to a halt at the reign of Edward I because there was so much to be prepared and explored before

[23] Fisher, *Maitland,* 2 f.
[24] *Pleas of the Crown for the County of Gloucester, 1221; Bracton's Note-Book; Select Pleas of the Crown, Vol. I, 1200–1225; Select Pleas in Manorial and Other Seignorial Courts, Vol. I, Reign of Henry III and Edward I.*
[25] *The English Village Community.*
[26] George Burton Adams, James F. Baldwin, Adolphus Ballard, Mary Bateson, and Helen Cam, to name only a few of those who will be pointed out in the following chapters.
[27] *Township and Borough.*

a synthesis could be produced. He turned to decipher the Year Books, but found it necessary to prepare a grammar of Norman French before he could proceed. He probably overestimated the value of the Year Books, but even this conclusion could not be reached before he and others had laid the groundwork by their investigations.[28]

Professor Schuyler tells us that Maitland has meant more to him than any other historian, "not primarily for the subjects he dealt with, but for his methods, his insights, and his superb historical sense.[29] Maitland also set a standard for scholarship in reviewing the work of another author. If a scholar is to persuade those of his readers who are really worth convincing, he must give them not bare theories but "the very terms of the original documents candidly, accurately, and at length."[30] Maitland practiced what he preached in this regard, for his works contain many Latin citations and his footnotes are liberally sprinkled with Latin quotations. This method precludes any concern for historical philosophy by its dedication to historical truth. Nor was Maitland content when he merely used documents, for these documents must be subjected to rigid examination. It was by this method that he determined that the Year Books were not official records maintained by the court but were the notebooks of young law students who were attending the court sessions.[31] In a similar

28 "Maitland once wrote that 'it will some day seem a wonderful thing that men once thought that they could write the history of England without using the Year Books.' That dictum has with reason been made the subject of controversy."—George O. Sayles, *Select Cases in the Court of King's Bench under Edward I*, III, cxii. This subject will be developed in Chapter VIII below.

29 "Historical Spirit Incarnate," *AHR*, Vol. LVII (1952), 303.

30 Maitland's review of Charles Gross's *The Gild Merchant*, in *Collected Papers*, II, 224.

31 *Year Books of Edward II* (3 vols., 1903-1905), III, xii.

manner he became convinced that Henry II, by the Assize of Clarendon, instituted the inquest or the presentment jury.[32] Henceforth, a jury could be summoned when there was no litigation in order to provide the king with desired information.

In little more than twenty years, and with Maitland severely hampered half the time by pleurisy, "a flood of books, articles, and reviews flowed from his pen, of a sustained high quality and, at times, brilliance unequalled in English historiography." "He left no rough edges and he touched nothing he did not adorn."[33] A recent editor of Maitland's essays remarked that "nothing that he wrote can ever be tarnished by time in the matchless attraction of his style or in the brilliant scholarship and originality of thought which he brought to bear upon every topic that he handled."[34] The writing style of Maitland would never rival that of Macaulay, Trevelyan, or Churchill in popular appeal, for two reasons. In the first place, the subject matter which formed the basis of his conclusions was of little interest to any but lawyers and scholars; and secondly, he was not writing for the masses. Nevertheless, he was able to express himself simply, clearly, and forcefully. His article in the *Cambridge Modern History* revealed that he was capable of writing for a much wider audience when he pleased.

Maitland's work as a researcher and editor enabled him to bring to his writing "that firmness of hand which nothing but original research can give."[35] Since his conclusions are based so squarely upon his sources, they cannot be ignored regard-

[32] *History of English Law*, I, 137–40.

[33] Ault, "The Maitland-Bigelow Letters," *Boston University Law Review,* Vol. XXXVII (1957), 286; G. P. Gooch, *History and Historians in the Nineteenth Century*, 373.

[34] *Selected Essays*, vii.

[35] Edward Fry's review of Pollock and Maitland's *History of English Law*, *EHR*, Vol. X (1895), 760.

less of their validity. It was his firm conviction that a good work of scholarship should possess value even though all of the conclusions of the writer should prove to be false.[36] The keenness of Maitland's mind and the originality of his thought are evident in most of his writings. His works are permeated with suggestions which deserve, and in many cases have received, close examination and further exposition. As was to be expected, some of his suggestions have proved to be fruitful[37] while others have fallen by the wayside.[38] The originality of his thought and the soundness of his scholarship are undoubtedly two of the outstanding characteristics discovered in his writings.

"The best of gamekeepers is a converted poacher, and the best historians of law have been converted lawyers."[39] The same qualities of mind which made him admirably suited to be a solicitor stood him in good stead in his approach to the history of law.[40] Maitland's ability to analyze is revealed in his effort to decipher the nature of the organization of the institutions of Anglo-Saxon society from the evidence of the

[36] Maitland's review of *The Gild Merchant*, in *Collected Papers*, II, 224.

[37] This is particularly true of his introduction to the Parliamentary Roll of 1305, which he edited for the Rolls Series. His suggestion that Parliament was a court before it was a legislature has been developed by Charles H. McIlwain in *The High Court of Parliament*. Other of Maitland's suggestions concerning Parliament and the central law courts embodied in this introduction and their development by other scholars are discussed in Chapters II and III below.

[38] Maitland's theory for the garrisoning of the ancient boroughs, which he suggested in *Domesday Book and Beyond*, is no longer accepted.

[39] Smith, *Maitland . . . Bibliography*, 32.

[40] "Every opinion that he gave was a complete legal essay, starting from first principles, showing how the question agreed with one, and disagreed with another, series of decisions and finally coming to a conclusion with the clearest grasp of legal points and the utmost lucidity of expression." Quoted from a letter of B. S. Rogers to H. A. L. Fisher.—Fisher, *Maitland*, 16.

Domesday survey.[41] His analytical mind was aware of the value, if not the necessity, of comparing English with Continental developments. He noted that during the reign of Henry II, England took the lead among the states of Europe "in the production of law and of a national legal literature." Next, he went on to contrast Glanvill's treatise with the absence of any counterpart in either Germany or France. In yet another place, he pointed out that English medieval law could be illustrated at numberless points by the contemporary law of France and Germany.[42] The comparative method held an important place in both Maitland's mind and his writings. His analytical skill is well exemplified in "The History of a Cambridgeshire Manor," in which he sets forth the chronological development of the manor of Wilburton belonging to the church of Ely from about 1350 through the sixteenth century. His highly developed powers of synthesis can be illustrated by his description of a typical manor, which he summarizes as follows:

> Thus we may regard the typical manor (1) as being *qua* vill, an unit of public law, of police and fiscal law, (2) as being an unit in the system of agriculture, (3) as being an unit in the management of property, (4) as being a judicial unit. But we have now to see that hardly one of these traits can be considered as absolutely essential.[43]

The quest for historical truth was uppermost in Maitland's scholarship. He tried to divest himself of all prejudice and preconceptions and so lose himself in the documents of the

[41] This thought is suggested by A. L. Smith in *Maitland . . . Bibliography*, 6.
[42] *History of English Law*, I, 167–68; "The Materials for English Legal History," *Collected Papers*, II, 4.
[43] *History of English Law*, I, 596 f.

period he was studying that he would be able to think the thoughts of medieval men after them. Professor Schuyler went so far as to declare, "I doubt whether any medievalist has ever made a more earnest and sustained effort to get inside the medieval mind."[44] Maitland's constant and relatively successful effort to approach the sources with an open mind led him to see many things which others had missed and to challenge beliefs which others had uncritically accepted. It was while reading the *Provinciale* of William Lyndwood[45] that Maitland became aware of a contradiction between the ideas of this fifteenth-century churchman and those attributed to fifteenth-century churchmen by the *Report of the Ecclesiastical Courts Commission.*[46] Maitland's lack of enthusiasm for any particular church or theological position gave him an impartiality and an open-mindedness which was generally not to be found in church historians. He was able to document and support his conclusions so satisfactorily that even Bishop Stubbs, who had helped in the preparation of the Report, accepted his conclusions.[47]

The quest for historical truth must involve thoughts as well as words. Maitland not only was a clear thinker but possessed an unusual knack of turning a clever phrase and, with a characteristic wit, driving home the point which would clinch his argument:

If we speak, we must speak with words; if we think, we must think with thoughts. We are moderns and our words and

[44] "Historical Spirit Incarnate," *AHR*, Vol. LVII (1952), 304.

[45] Lyndwood finished his glosses of the provincial constitutions of the Archbishop of Canterbury in 1430. Maitland used the Oxford edition of 1679.

[46] This report was published in 1883. Bishop Stubbs wrote a historical introduction to it in which he accepted the Anglican position of the medieval origin of a distinct Anglican church and law.

[47] "Frederick William Maitland," *D.N.B. Supplement 1901–1911,* 553.

thoughts can not but be modern. Perhaps, as Mr. Gilbert once suggested, it is too late for us to be early English. Every thought will be too sharp, every word will imply too many contrasts. We must, it is to be feared, use many words and qualify our every statement until we have almost contradicted it.[48]

His concern for truth inevitably led to extreme care in his choice and use of words in order that he might convey the exact sense or meaning that he had grasped. This has made it relatively easy for those who have differed with him to take issue with him, for no one has ever professed ignorance of the meaning or intention of Maitland's words. "Maitland's ear for gradations in the scale of meaning was extraordinarily sensitive; it would be difficult, in any of his writings, to find cases of semantic flatting or sharping."[49] His daughter tells us that he was very careful in dealing with words and always said or thought the words to himself as he read or wrote. He even went so far as to recite his lectures to himself as he paced back and forth, in order to make certain that what he said sounded as he intended that it should.[50] One of the qualities which contributed most to attract his readers was the "wealth of humor that pervaded all his writings, in spite of their severe aims and their highly technical details."[51] One cannot read Maitland's writings for very long without coming across one of his "happy pointed phrases." His humor is not an ornamental adjunct but generally concludes an argument in which he sums up his case in the manner of "a wise and kindly judge who takes into account all the extenuating circumstances and as he looks at the culprit feels 'there, but for the grace of God,

[48] *Township and Borough*, 22.
[49] Schuyler, "Historical Spirit Incarnate," *AHR*, Vol. LVII (1952), 320.
[50] Ermengard Maitland, *A Child's-Eye View*, 8.
[51] Paul Vinogradoff, "Maitland's Literary Style," *Maitland Reader*, 188.

stands Richard Baxter.' "[52] His introduction to *Mirror of Justices*[53] is probably the best extended example of his use of humor in effectively handling an involved and complicated problem involving the book's authorship, purpose, and value.[54]

After a decade of private law practice, Maitland, in 1884, returned to Cambridge as a Reader of English Law. The publication of *Pleas of the Crown for the County of Gloucester* earlier in the year had won for him wide recognition as a scholar. He was to remain at Cambridge first as Reader and then as Downing Professor of the Laws of England for the remainder of his life. He confided to his friend Vinogradoff on many occasions "that he would much rather devote his life to the historical study of English law than watch his chamber in Lincoln's Inn for footsteps of the client who never comes."[55] Maitland had attracted the attention of Frederick Pollock as early as 1879 when Maitland published an article on "The Law of Real Property."[56] Pollock found in Maitland a kindred mind; and a friendship developed, which, among other things, resulted in the *History of English Law*.

Soon after settling at Cambridge, Maitland recognized that his vision of writing the history of English law was so broad that a co-operative effort would be required to do the editing and produce the monographs which would form the foundation for such a work. He therefore instituted the organization of the Selden Society in 1887 "to encourage the study and advance the knowledge of the history of English law." It has

[52] Smith, *Maitland . . . Bibliography,* 21, 20.
[53] *The Mirror of Justices,* ed. by Joseph William Whittaker, with an introduction by F. W. Maitland.
[54] Smith, *Maitland . . . Bibliography,* 21.
[55] Vinogradoff, "Maitland," *EHR,* Vol. XXII (1907), 280.
[56] Gooch, *History and Historians in the Nineteenth Century,* 367–68.

been said that without Maitland's genius, learning, and devotion the Selden Society would not have existed.[57] There is no question but that he was its prime mover, and he was its first literary editor. Eight of the twenty-one volumes issued by the society during his lifetime came from his pen,[58] and another was almost completed at his death.[59] "Of the rest every sheet passed under his supervision either in manuscript or in proof, and often in both."[60] ". . . his introductions to his own volumes have been a boon to students because of his lucid presentation of his findings, his clear-visioned insights, his original and ingenious hypotheses, and his critical methods."[61]

Maitland was not only a scholar but also a professor. His inheritance of a modest estate from his grandfather enabled him not only to marry in 1886 while living on the slender stipend of a Reader but also to "incur the expense involved in the preparation and publication of some of his most important work."[62] We know of his lectures through both the witness of his students and posthumous publication.[63] As Miss Cam

---

[57] Fisher, *Maitland*, 52.

[58] *Select Pleas of the Crown*, Vol. I, *1200–1225*; *Select Pleas in Manorial and Other Seignorial Courts*; *The Court Baron*, in collaboration with W. P. Baildon; *The Mirror of Justices*, ed. by W. J. Whittaker, with an introduction by Maitland; *Selected Passages from the Works of Bracton and Azo*; *Year Books of Edward II*, Vol. I, *1307–1309*; *Year Books of Edward II*, *1308–1309*, *1309–1310*; *Year Books of Edward II*, *1309–1310*.

[59] *Year Books of Edward II*, *1309–1311*, ed. by F. W. Maitland and G. J. Turner.

[60] Benjamin Fossett Lock, "Maitland," *Solicitors' Journal* (January 5, 1907), quoted in Fisher, *Maitland*, 53.

[61] Schuyler, "The Historical Spirit Incarnate," *AHR*, Vol. LVII (1952), 308.

[62] *Bracton's Note-book*; Henry Arthur Hollond, "F. W. Maitland, 1850–1906: A Memorial Address," *Selden Society Annual Lecture* (1953), reprinted in *Maitland Reader*, 13.

[63] *The Constitutional History of England*, ed. by H. A. L. Fisher; *Equity; Also the Forms of Action at Common Law*, ed. by A. H. Chaytor and W. J. Whittaker.

has pointed out, it is to be regretted that Maitland is known to so many students mainly through his lectures on constitutional history which were written in 1888 and published after his death against his declared judgment. His lectures had the same general characteristics which distinguished his writings. They were "original, illuminating, suggestive, and stimulating in what they had to say, which was carefully prepared"[64] and read in a slow, distinct voice which enabled the student to take full notes. Maitland did not shirk his non-teaching professorial duties, but carried them out with the same thoroughness and loyalty that marked his other academic activities.

Maitland's chief impact upon the teaching of history was "his presentation of Henry II as founder of the common law, and with it of the English monarchy as the guardian of justice to all."[65] Today it is universally recognized that Maitland's introduction to the Parliamentary Roll of 1305 is equally original. Although it appeared in 1893, it attracted little attention until 1910, when Charles McIlwain's *High Court of Parliament* appeared. The implications and suggestions of Maitland's introduction have produced a major revision in the accepted views on the nature and the origin of Parliament. This introduction is an outstanding example of Maitland's critical approach to his documents. It seems strange that he did not return to this subject, but his failure to do so might be explained by suggesting that he considered it to be a constitutional rather than a legal issue and therefore outside the realm of his prime concern. The failure of scholars to grasp the implications of this introduction—that the history of Parliament must be rewritten—may be attributed to the seeming tentativeness of Maitland's approach.[66] In only one instance

[64] Schuyler, "The Historical Spirit Incarnate," *AHR*, Vol. LVII (1952), 308.
[65] Cam, in *Historical Essays*, xv.
[66] *Ibid.*, xvii.

did he suggest that he had ventured to differ from what seemed to be the general opinion of scholars, and he even questioned whether this difference was real or apparent.[67] At the time that Maitland wrote, it was necessary to emphasize the curial nature of Parliament. Those who pursued this course, including Maitland himself, underestimated the political aspects of a parliament. We are now able to obtain a more balanced estimate of the nature and function of Parliament than was possible heretofore.

Maitland's character and personality are reflected in the reviews which he wrote of the works of others and by his own reactions to what others said or wrote about his own work. His judgments on the writings of others were as astute as those which he made on the documents that formed the basis of his own writings. He had a critical mind which enabled him to read with insight, and yet even his criticisms usually reflected a kindliness of manner. He was called upon to write reviews of thirty-three books, mostly for the *English Historical Review.* He declined the invitation of Reginald L. Poole to review other books because of personal feelings about their authors.[68] Maitland began his reviews by pointing out the strong points or major contributions of the work under consideration before mentioning its shortcomings. He was never afraid to state what appeared to him to be the truth merely because it went against accepted opinion; in fact, he seemed to take delight in challenging views which were hallowed by tradition. His manner was entirely different, however, when it came to deal-

---

[67] "Introduction to *Memoranda de Parliamento,*" *Selected Essays,* 71, n. 1.

[68] Hubert Hall's edition of *The Red Book of the Exchequer,* published for the Rolls Series in 1896. J. H. Round in reviewing this book criticized Hall severely. The review led to a bitter controversy which became personal between Round and Maitland. A. L. Poole, "Letters from Maitland to R. L. Poole," *CHJ,* Vol. X (1952), 325, n. 33.

ing with individuals. Although he set forth his revisionary views concerning English canon law in a forthright manner, he was disturbed when he heard that Bishop Stubbs had taken personal offense at his words. Maitland's views on English canon law were first revealed in a series of articles in the *English Historical Review*. As he was bringing his essays together to republish them in book form, he wrote to Reginald Poole:

> I hope and trust that you were not very serious when you said that the Bishop was "sore." I feel for him a respect so deep that if you told me that the republication of my essays would make him more unhappy than a sane man is whenever people dissent from him, I should be in great doubt what to do. It is not too late to destroy all or some of the sheets. I hate to bark at the heels of a great man whom I admire but tried to seem, as well as to be, respectful.[69]

When it came to having his own work reviewed, Maitland preferred to have the most competent critic examine it. In submitting two of the volumes which he prepared for the Selden Society to the *English Historical Review—The Mirror of Justices* and *Bracton and Azo*—he asked that a professed Romanist be asked to review them. He disclaimed any knowledge of Roman law and wanted to know "whether I have been guilty of many 'howlers'—in short I want to know the worst."[70] But he was not one to sit idly by while his works were subjected to an ill-founded attack. The Reverend Malcolm MacColl, canon of Ripon, entered into controversy with Maitland on the subject of canon law. Maitland's reply was a devastating one which removed the Anglican position from serious con-

[69] Letter to Poole, September 12, 1898, *ibid.*
[70] Letter to Poole, July 15, 1895, *ibid.*

tention thereafter.[71] Round took exception to some of the views expressed in *Domesday Book and Beyond*.[72] but this did not upset Maitland's equilibrium, for he recognized the weakness of his position. In a letter to Poole, he wrote: "It grieves me that you should brood over my Domesday. Of all that I have written that makes me most uncomfortable. I try to cheer myself by saying that I have given others a lot to contradict."[73] Earlier, he had taken the unusual steps of writing a letter to James Tait concerning the latter's review of *Domesday Book and Beyond*. In it he expressed his appreciation for the critical nature of the review, which went far toward establishing Tait's reputation as one of the best historical scholars in England.[74] This was typical of Maitland's encouragement to young scholars. Professor W. W. Buckland pointed out that Maitland was tolerant of slips and even ignorances in a younger scholar and illustrated the point by relating a personal experience.[75]

The British educational system of Maitland's day did not place great emphasis upon what today we should call graduate study; therefore, Maitland's lectures were directed primarily toward undergraduates who were preparing for the Tripos. This system had two effects upon Maitland which were different from what his experience would have been had he been teaching in either the United States or Germany. First, he had few students whom he could prepare to assist him in his work or to follow him in realizing the vision which no man

---

[71] *Fortnightly Review* (October, 1899); "Canon MacColl's New Convocation," *Fortnightly Review* (December, 1899), reprinted in *Collected Papers*, III, 119–37.

[72] *EHR*, Vol. XII (1897), 492; *ibid.*, Vol. XV (1900), 78, 293.

[73] August 26, 1900, *CHJ*, Vol. X (1952), 329 f.

[74] Reprinted in Powicke, *Modern Historians*, 55 f.

[75] "F. W. Maitland," *Cambridge Law Journal*, Vol. I (1923), reprinted in the *Maitland Reader*, 36 f.

could complete in one lifetime. Nevertheless, he did hold a few advanced classes in paleography and diplomatics for the study of medieval English charters. He contended that in sixty hours he could train a student to read medieval documents with "fluency and exactitude."[76] Second, Maitland was not the founder of any formal "school" although his views on the Parliament of 1305 are often considered the beginning of a distinct school of thought upon that subject.[77] Mary Bateson was the only pupil of his who followed directly in her master's footsteps, but unfortunately her untimely death preceded Maitland's. Her industry and judgment rivaled that of Maitland. Her scholarship and her work as an editor brought her recognition as one of the best medievalists in England, and for this she gave credit to the "counsel and direction of Professor Maitland."[78]

Maitland certainly had a broad vision of the history of English law. He expressed the hope that he would be able to bring "the English law of the thirteenth century into line with the French and German law of the same age." He felt that it would be impossible to evaluate adequately the true character of English law apart from the larger context of European law. He took pains to try to determine what was known to Glanvill and Bracton, but he was equally interested in contemporary scholarship among French, German, and American scholars. He indicated that he was trying to do for English law what many had already done for French and German law. He seemed to be one of the first English scholars to appreciate the work of American scholars. He was instrumental in getting Bige-

[76] In 1892, 1894, 1903, 1904, and 1905.—Fisher, *Maitland,* 171.

[77] Robert S. Hoyt, "Recent Publications in the United States and Canada on the History of Representative Institutions before the French Revolution," *Speculum,* Vol. XXIX (1954), 356–77.

[78] *Borough Customs,* I.

low's book on *Torts* accepted in his law school and even an English edition of it published by the Cambridge University Press.[79] Perhaps it was Maitland's early appreciation of American scholars which contributed in part at least to acclaim of him among scholars in the United States. He corresponded with several American professors and received them when they visited England.

The breadth of Maitland's vision for his subject explains why he was not able to complete the exposition of the history of English law. When he began his study, he carried the account back to Anglo-Saxon times on the strength of his Domesday studies and the research of other experts on local history. Maitland himself contributed a history of ancient Cambridge.[80] He was able to carry his account forward to the time of the beginning of the Year Books. He felt that a critical edition of the Year Books was essential to the carrying forward of his main interest. This could not be done without a thorough knowledge of the Anglo-Norman French in which the records were made. Maitland investigated this language so thoroughly that a contemporary philologist, M. Paul Meyer, recommended his introduction to the first volume of the *Year Books of Edward II* to all students of medieval French.[81]

Thus far, we have been endeavoring to gain an insight into Maitland's mind, methods, and concepts of history. In the

[79] *History of English Law*, I, *xxv, xxvi;* letter to Bigelow, October 7, 1886, *Boston University Law Review*, Vol. XXXVII (1957), 289. Cambridge University Press published an edition of Bigelow's *Torts* in 1889. It was dedicated "to my Friends F. W. Maitland and R. T. Wright."—Ault, "The Maitland-Bigelow Letters," *Boston University Law Review*, Vol. XXXVII (1957), 294, n. 19.

[80] *Township and Borough* was based largely on Cambridge documents, as was "The History of a Cambridgeshire Manor," *EHR*, Vol. IX (1894), 417–39.

[81] Pollock, "Maitland," *LQR*, Vol. XXIII (1907), reprinted in the *Maitland Reader*, 27.

remaining chapters of this work a detailed examination of his contributions to the history of English law will be made in an effort not only to learn what his contributions were fifty years ago but also to determine which of his conclusions are still accepted and which have been modified or abandoned.

II

MEMORANDA

DE PARLIAMENTO

MAITLAND'S VIEWS on the subject of Parliament in the time of Edward I are to be found primarily in his introduction to the *Memoranda de Parliamento*.[1] It seems a bit surprising that he wrote so little upon this subject. After having raised large issues which would invite a departure from the accepted teachings, he apparently lost interest in the problem. Parliament is barely mentioned in the *History of English Law*. Although this history purports to end "before the time of Edward I," many important things which might have been said about Parliament in the time of Henry III have been left unsaid. It is as though Maitland had placed "a question mark in the margin of some pages of Stubbs' *Constitutional History* and had been content."[2]

As he edited this volume for the Rolls Series, Maitland, of necessity, had to determine, at least for his own satisfaction, the nature of the Parliament for the year 1305 on the basis of documents which lay before him. It certainly must have

[1] F. W. Maitland (ed.), *Records of the Parliament Holden at Westminster, on the 28th Day of February, 1305.*

[2] H. G. Richardson and G. O. Sayles, *The Irish Parliament in the Middle Ages,* 3 f.

occurred to him that the observations which he has recorded for us in his introduction did not coincide with the accepted views on the character of Parliament. And yet he declared that on only one point did he "venture to differ from what seems to be the general opinion of modern historians (and I am uncertain as to whether this difference is real) . . . ."[3]

Maitland made a singular contribution to the understanding of the Parliament of Edward I, but before considering what this contribution actually was, we must offer a word of caution against making extreme claims on his behalf. In the first place, he was not the first to challenge the orthodox concept of Parliament. In 1885, Ludwig Riess published a work entitled *Geschichte des Wahlrects zum englischen Parlament in Mittelalter*. This was followed by an article in *Historische Zeitschrift* on the origin of the "House of Commons," in which Riess discussed the reasons why Edward I first summoned representatives of the boroughs and shires to Parliament.[4] Maitland knew of Riess's work and is known to have owned a copy of the *Geschichte des Wahlrects*, which is now in the Cambridge University Library.

In an editorial note to Maitland's introduction to the *Memoranda de Parliamento*, Mr. Lapsley suggests that when this introduction appeared, "the orthodox doctrine of Hallam, Gneist, and Stubbs still held the field."[5] In reading through Stubbs' *Constitutional History* to learn the "orthodox doctrine," I found myself questioning the implications of Mr. Lapsley's statement. There is no question but that the outlook and spirit of Maitland and Stubbs are very different; but, as we shall see, the basic difference is one of emphasis and

[3] Maitland, "Introduction to *Memoranda de Parliamento*," *Selected Essays*, 71.
[4] *"Der Ursprung des englischen Unterhauses,"* in Vol. LX (1888), 1–33.
[5] *Selected Essays*, 2.

interpretation, not disagreement concerning the elements which comprise Parliament. Maitland set forth his observations in a forthright manner with no apparent preconceived theory or philosophy. Yet it seems to me that Stubbs in his conservative way at least pointed in the direction which the investigation of Maitland took. Stubbs' research paved the way for such historians as Maitland, Round, and G. B. Adams, who were to break down "the nationalist theory" of the origins of the English constitution.[6]

At the time that Maitland edited the roll of Parliament for the year 1305, English historical scholarship was still dominated by the prevalent ideas of the nineteenth century. Although a more scientific approach to the study of history had appeared in the seminars of the German universities, this approach had made little headway in England. Historians were still strongly nationalistic and were prone to read the democratic ideas of nineteenth-century Britain back into earlier times, where, in fact, these ideas did not exist. Although Stubbs was one of the foremost historians of his day because of his considered judgment and his practice of basing his conclusions upon documentary evidence, he was nevertheless influenced by the ideas of his age. Stubbs' *Constitutional History* was generally accepted as the standard authority upon the subject matter with which it dealt until it was challenged directly or indirectly by such writers as Maitland and Round.

For Stubbs, the Parliament of Edward I combined two distinct principles which form the basis of the modern governmental system in England. The first of these was the principle of local machinery of government embodied in a system of parliamentary representation. This was distinctly local repre-

6 J. F. Baldwin, *The King's Council in England During the Middle Ages*, 2.

sentation as opposed to class representation. Secondly, he could see in England the system of estates which was common to most of Western Europe. In England, "the three estates of clergy, lords, and commons, finally emerge as the political constituents of the nation, or, in their parliamentary form, as the lords spiritual and temporal and commons."

The year 1295 fixed finally and for all time "the right of shire and town representation, although for a few years the system admits of some modifications." The parliament of 1295 became indeed a "model parliament" for Stubbs. Perhaps there was some question about who should attend Parliament before 1295, but there certainly could be no question thereafter. The writs for assembling the representatives addressed to the sheriffs directed the election "not of the knights but of citizens and burghers" in the county courts.

As we shall see, Stubbs represents a different approach to the history of Parliament from that taken by Maitland. We have noted that Bishop Stubbs was not able to divorce his thinking about the origins of the government which he loved so dearly from the concepts which it embodied in his own day. In fairness, we must realize that the source material upon which Maitland and others based their conclusions had become far more accessible than when Stubbs and other mid-nineteenth-century historians produced their works. Yet we find that when Stubbs ceased to make broad generalizations and went to sources for details on Parliament, there is much less to which to take exception.

Under Edward I, the parliament of "prelates and barons had been asked for and had granted aids, had given counsel and consent to legislation, had acted as a supreme court of justice, and had discussed questions of foreign policy and internal administration." Stubbs acknowledged the fact that the

King had, and exercised, the right to do without Parliament anything that he did with its counsel and consent. The king, however, seldom chose to act completely upon his own initiative, usually relying upon the advice and consent of his council. The king in his council at the time of Edward I could legally do anything that the king in his Parliament could do. "The opposition between the royal and national councils, between the privy council and the parliament, is an important element in later national history."[7]

According to the "orthodox view," from the time of Edward I the task of the constitutional historian was to examine this struggle between the king's council and Parliament to determine "whether any given act or policy was or was not 'constitutional' by reference to the institutional work of Edward I and the principles which animated it."[8] Ludwig Riess preceded Maitland in raising a note of protest against this view, held by Stubbs in England and Gneist in Germany. Referring to Parliament in the time of Edward I, Riess wrote:

> As yet the commons had no common rights, and no corporate duties: the right of granting taxes had not been conceded to them, legislation was not dependent on their assent, a directing influence over the central government was entirely outside the sphere of their activities. No wonder that the election to such a national assembly attracted little attention.[9]

Although Maitland was not the first to challenge the orthodox position, he seems to have been the one to whom most later writers have given credit for suggesting revisions of the former

---

[7] *Constitutional History of England*, II, 169, 174, 251, 235, 252.
[8] *Selected Essays*, 2.
[9] Ludwig Riess, *The History of the English Electoral Law in the Middle Ages*, 76.

ideas.[10] It was not long before the views which Maitland expressed in this introduction became the new orthodoxy and formed the basis for a whole new school in the interpretation of Parliament.[11]

The Parliament of 1305 was a "full parliament in our sense of that term."[12] For Maitland this meant that the three estates of the realm met the king and his council. This view has been successfully challenged and is no longer generally held. Pollard has suggested that "full" may be a mistranslation of Latin on account of the fact that the Latin word itself is a translation from the French. *"In pleno parliamento* stands for *en plein parlement,"* but the French word means "open" instead of "full."[13] Even in the session of 1305 which we are considering, Parliament remained full or in open session after the representative elements had departed.

This parliamentary assembly sat for three weeks. At the end of this time the King issued a proclamation telling all who were not members of the council to go home. Members of the king's council and those who still had unfinished business

[10] While I probably have not found everything written upon the subject, nowhere have I found credit given to Riess even when his name is mentioned. It was Maitland who first publicized the revision, and he has been followed principally by McIlwain and Richardson and Sayles. Cf. Geoffrey Templeman in "The History of Parliament to 1400 in the Light of Modern Research," *University of Birmingham Historical Journal,* Vol. I (1948), 202–31 (reprinted in *The Making of English History,* ed. by R. L. Schuyler and H. Ausubel). "In the long run the views expressed in the introduction to this work [*Memoranda de Parliamento*] did more to outmode Stubbs' theory of Medieval parliamentary history than any other single contribution to the subject."—*The Making of English History,* 114.

[11] In an article in *Speculum* (Vol. XXIX [1954]), "Recent Publications in the United States and Canada on the History of Representative Institutions before the French Revolution," Professor Hoyt refers several times to the "Maitland–McIlwain–Richardson and Sayles School." I agree wholeheartedly with this reference.

[12] "Introduction to *Memoranda de Parliamento," Selected Essays,* 14.

[13] A. F. Pollard, *The Evolution of Parliament,* 33.

were required to remain. The parliamentary roll for this session records transactions of business after the representative elements of this parliament had gone home.[14] Maitland merely records this observation without comment or elaboration. It is one of the reasons why his introduction is considered to be such a suggestive essay. We may readily draw the conclusion for ourselves that the representative element was not essential for the functioning of Parliament. The representative element, as we shall see, added to the taxing power of the assembly, but it apparently added nothing to its legislative or judicial authority. It has been stated that "the great legislative enactments of Edward I were not even promulgated in a representative assembly."[15]

One of today's leading authorities upon the subject of Parliament corroborates our conclusion:

> It is from the standpoint of the modern age that the feeble beginnings of popular representation have any importance in parliamentary history: in the thirteenth century the popular element is of little significance, so far at least as the competence, jurisdiction or procedure of parliament is concerned.[16]

The council of Edward I was, for Maitland, "an ill-defined group of men."[17] In an attempt to ascertain the membership of Edward's council, Maitland examined the signatures of the witnesses to the King's charters. It was apparent that certain men accompanied the King more frequently than others, but this does not determine for us who was or who was not

---

[14] "Introduction to *Memoranda de Parliamento,*" *Selected Essays,* 14 ff.
[15] Pollard, *The Evolution of Parliament,* 33 f.
[16] H. G. Richardson, "The Origins of Parliament," *Transactions of the Royal Historical Society,* Fourth Series, Vol. XI (1928), 168 f.
[17] "Introduction to *Memoranda de Parliamento,*" *Selected Essays,* 15.

definitely a member of the king's council. Maitland could only conclude:

> We may well believe that according to the notions of this age the king has a clear right to call upon any one of his subjects to give him counsel; and bold would have been the man who either refused to come, or who refused to sit beside any one whom he found at the council board. This makes it exceedingly hard for us to say that one man is while another man is not a permanent councillor.[18]

The King's council was undoubtedly feudal in origin, although its origin cannot be ascribed to any given point in time, for it grew out of the prevailing feudal idea that the king, like any other lord, was accustomed to receive the "aid and counsel" of his vassals.[19] "Counsellors were a strength in peace because they were a necessity in war."[20] It is difficult for us of the twentieth century to divest ourselves of the idea of nations and nationalism, but these concepts do not enter into either the ideas or the institutions of the medieval period. The king was not compelled to accept and act upon the advice of his councillors, but, on the other hand, he did not feel free to disregard it completely. The realm was to be regarded as the king's private fief. He administered the feudal law of the fief. There was far more law-declaring than law-making in the early medieval period. It came to be understood that if the king desired to make innovations in the feudal law, he must consult his subjects.[21]

The leading authority on the king's council contends that

18 *Ibid.*, 25.
19 Baldwin, *The King's Council*, 3.
20 McIlwain, *The High Court of Parliament*, 9 f.
21 George L. Haskins, *The Growth of English Representative Government*, 31.

it emerged with a permanent character during the minority of Henry III. It was not a new creation at this time but merely a "quickening and adaptation of the consilium" to the new situation. During the early years of Henry III, the government was by council as completely as it could be.[22] A study of the indices of the *curia regis* rolls will show a great increase in the quantity of business which came before the council during the reigns of John and Henry III. The council could exercise executive, judicial, or legislative functions without any discrimination.

Maitland declared that the one point in his introduction on which he dared to differ from the prevailing opinions of the leading historians of his day concerned the *consilium* of Edward I. It was generally believed that there were distinctions among *commune concilium, magnum concilium, concilium ordinarium, parliamentum,* etc. It was Maitland's contention that the king's council embraced all of these. "A full meeting of the council is a full meeting of the king's bench, of the common bench, of the chancery, of the exchequer; it is all this and more than this." The issue is complicated by the absence of either the definite or the indefinite article in Latin and by the indifference with which medieval clerks interchanged *concilium* and *consilium*.[23] It is certain that at some times there were more men attending the council than at others. One of Maitland's disciples has carried his point of view to its ultimate conclusion. If at these times it was called the *magnum concilium,* it was not a "distinct body, separate in function, in organization and in rights . . . ."[24] Further study has resulted in a modification of this position. Only in the case

22 Baldwin, *The King's Council*, 16, 21, 19.
23 "Introduction to *Memoranda de Parliamento," Selected Essays,* 71 n. 1; 27; Pollard, *The Evolution of Parliament*, 28.
24 McIlwain, *The High Court of Parliament*, 17.

of the *magnum concilium,* however, has Maitland's contention been successfully challenged.[25] The well-known and highly regarded medievalist, Lady Stenton, summarizes the currently accepted point of view:

> That such a body as a select council, in addition to the great council of the king's tenants in chief, was a necessity no one doubted. The complexity of affairs with which the crown must deal . . . demanded the best brains of the time. It was need which brought and kept this select council in being.[26]

The business of medieval parliaments is usually grouped under five main headings: (1) the discussion of important affairs of state, which usually in this period mean foreign affairs; (2) legislation or changes in the law; (3) taxation or supply; (4) the hearing of petitions from individuals, groups, and, less frequently, the elected representatives of the boroughs and shires in commons assembled; and, finally, (5) judicial business, both civil and criminal. It is on the basis of the records or rolls of Parliament that we must determine what Parliament could do by observing what, in fact, it did do. With this outline in mind, let us now turn to the roll of the Parliament of 1305 to compare a concrete example with a theoretical outline.

The summons to the Parliament of 1305 stated that the King wished to treat "of certain matters specially touching our realm of England and the establishment of our land of

[25] Pollard contends that if we can find little about a Great Council under Edward I, at least "we can read a great deal about it under Henry III and Edward II."—*The Evolution of Parliament,* 29. Richardson and Sayles regard the term "great council" as one marking a distinction of practical importance ("Parliaments of Edward III," *Bulletin of the Institute of Historical Research* [hereafter BIHR], Vol. VIII [1934], 72–73; "The King's Ministers in Parliament, *EHR,* Vol. XLVII [1932] 199–201).

[26] Doris Mary Stenton, *English Society in the Early Middle Ages,* 53.

Scotland." Edward called upon the Bishop of Glasgow, the Earl of Carrick, and John Mowbray to speak for Scotland regarding a representation at a parliament to be held later in the year. An interesting fact is that these men did not answer the King's question until after the representative elements had already gone home. Their reply was that two representatives from each segment of the Scottish society would be adequate: two bishops, two abbots, two earls, two barons, and two men elected by the community of Scotland. There is no specific reference to the King's discussing any matters of state with the representative elements at this parliament. There was much business on the affairs of Gascony, but this may have been the proper subject of discussion and advice for the council only; we are not able to determine. The king had had a dispute with Archbishop Winchelsea, but this matter may also have been the exclusive concern of the council rather than the assembly. It is Maitland's guess that the assembly probably spent much of its time discussing the general complaint that monks, especially Cistercians, were sending large sums of money out of the country to alien mother houses.[27] This was the subject of a petition presented to the King and his council by the elected elements, and the subject of petitions will be discussed later. We certainly cannot assume in this parliament, at least, that the real reason for summoning the representative element was to advise the King concerning affairs of the realm, although they may or may not have done so incidentally.

In the way of legislation, this parliament did little or nothing. There were no statutes entered upon the statute roll, althought there were some acts of a legislative character. The first of these is in the form of an answer to the petition concerning the revenues of monasteries. The parliamentary roll

[27] "Introduction to *Memoranda de Parliamento*," *Selected Essays*, 28, 29 ff.

introduces a statute, but a blank occurs where the statute should be found. Two years later the Statute of Carlisle *"De Asportis religiosorum"* is enacted or re-enacted on the same subject.[28] There were three more ordinances recorded for this parliament,[29] and the interesting thing, to me at least, is that each purports to be the answer to one or more petitions. Two of these[30] are issued in the King's name alone with no reference to either Parliament or the council, while the third[31] is issued in the name of the "king and his whole council." Maitland does not generalize upon the legislative functions of Parliament in general, but he has left a foundation for the further labors, elaborations, and discussions of others.

Although today it is generally held that the chief purpose of calling the representative elements to parliament was for the granting of supply, this factor seems strangely absent from the Parliament of 1305. There were, however, discussions, in three particulars, upon the subject of scutage and tallage. In each case a petition was presented to the King, and in each case he granted it.[32] In each of these cases, however, the peti-

[28] *Ibid.*, 31.

[29] "Ordinance of Inquests," *Statutes of the Realm*, I, 143; "Ordinatio Forestal," *Memoranda de Parliamento*, No. 10; and "Ordinatio de Trailbastions," *Parliamentary Writs*, I, 408. This last refers to a problem of this time when bands of robbers carrying sticks were hiding in the woods along the roadways to waylay travelers. Edward was attempting to suppress this brigandage.

[30] The forest ordinance and the ordinance of trail bastion.

[31] The ordinance of inquests.

[32] In the first case, "the bishops, abbots, earls, barons, and others of the realm," because of their military service in the Scottish campaign of 1300 and 1303, sought permission to take scutage from their tenants (*Memoranda de Parliamento*, No. 198). The laymen of the above group complained that the officers of the exchequer were assessing scutage even when military service had been rendered (*ibid.*, 203). In the third case, the "archbishops, bishops, prelates, earls, barons, and other good men of the land," noting that the King had recently tallaged his demesnes, asked permission to tallage that part of the ancient demesnes of the crown which were in their hands (*ibid.*, No. 87).

tioners were only asking for their just deserts, which could be gained in no other way. The chief activity of the Parliament of 1305 was the hearing of petitions. The largest section of Maitland's introduction was devoted to the discussion of this subject. Let us consider his principal contentions. Three weeks before the day fixed for the assembling of Parliament, Edward instructed his chancellor and treasurer to proclaim that all who had petitions to present "to us and our council at the forthcoming parliament" should present them to the prescribed receivers before a certain date. The King further desired that the petitions should be sorted and answered, so far as possible, through normal channels. No petitions were to come before the King in person except those which could not be "delivered" in any other way. In this parliament we see the appointment of "auditors of petitions" for Gascony, Scotland, and Ireland but apparently none for England. Maitland says that this is the first evidence we have of the appointment of any auditors. Some petitions were reserved for the King's eye or ear, and others were held for plenary meetings of the council. Maitland found written on the margin of some of the surviving petitions, *"coram rege,"* or *"coram consilio."* A distinction must be made between these petitions and the petitions of the Commons which were to occupy so large a part of the parliamentary rolls of Edward III's day. "Parliament" during the reign of Edward I still retained the original meaning of the word, a time for discussion, rather than the later idea of a body which could be petitioned. Most of these petitions were not of a nature to require discussion by a large assembly. Usually the request of the petitioner was a subject which came within the personal cognizance of the King or of one of his chosen administrators.[33]

[33] "Introduction to *Memoranda de Parliamento,*" *Selected Essays,* 35, 37, 41, 42, 47 f., 49.

Maitland accepts Hale's conclusion regarding the answers to these petitions: ". . . most of the answers that the council gave were in the nature of remissions of the petitions to those persons or courts that had properly the cognizance of the causes."[34] Maitland was forced to concede that beyond a very few items he could only guess at what the assembled commoners were doing during their three weeks at Westminster. While willing to admit that it could easily be pressed too far, he generally accepted the idea that the representatives of the shires and towns were called to assemble, not to act on behalf of the realm, but in order "to represent before the king in council the grievances and the interests of the particular community, county, or borough that sent them."[35]

Although Maitland next goes on to an examination of the judicial business of the Parliament, he quickly launches into a discussion of the whole system of central law courts. In this he goes over much of the same ground that he had covered in his earlier introduction to *Select Pleas of the Crown,* which will be developed in the next chapter. We must now further illustrate the basic contention of this chapter that Maitland's introductory essay has become the foundation for much of the investigation of the medieval parliament during the past sixty-five years.

There were undoubtedly several reasons for the King's call-

[34] *Jurisdiction,* 67 f., quoted by Maitland in his "Introduction to *Memoranda de Parliamento,*" *Selected Essays,* 50.

[35] *Ibid.,* 57. Maitland undoubtedly got this idea from the writings of Riess, referred to above. Riess suggested that it was the purpose of Edward I to summon representatives as a means of checking up on the sheriffs and to control local affairs better. The representatives were to bring petitions of their grievances to Parliament and take home the answers of the King in his council. Although Riess recognized that the King undoubtedly intended for the representatives to consent to revenues and thus aid in their collection, he emphasized the task of bringing petitions and reporting the replies.

ing for the selection of representatives of the boroughs and the shires to meet with him and his council in parliament. The opinion of Maitland cited above held the field for some time. It has been pointed out that Maitland's argument on this point was essentially negative since it was an argument from silence.[36] There seems to be no evidence to support his contention. Nevertheless, in the absence of an alternative interpretation, his conclusion was generally accepted.

At the time Maitland was writing, the majority of historians were interested primarily in political institutional history. Maitland's own concern, of course, was the history of English law. Social, intellectual, cultural, and economic considerations have come in for a much closer scrutiny in more recent years. Because of a broadening of interest in the subject matter of historical investigation, conclusions based upon the incomplete evidence in the last century must be modified and reevaluated in our own day. Most scholars now agree that although the representatives of the shires and boroughs could be of assistance in informing the king and his council on matters of local interest and of representing the desires and ideas of the central government on the local level, the need of the crown for revenue was the most important factor in the summoning of knights and burgesses to parliament.[37] As the feudal principles began to weaken under the centralizing tendencies of the government under a strong king such as Edward I, the magnates of the realm found it more difficult to pass on the real burden of taxation without consulting those who must

[36] George L. Haskins, "Petitions of Representatives in the Parliament of Edward I," *EHR*, Vol. LIII (1938), 15.

[37] J. G. Edwards, "The Personnel of the Commons in Parliament under Edward I and Edward II," *Essays in Medieval History*, 147; Carl Stephenson, "Taxation and Representation," in *Haskins Anniversary Essays*, 311–12, n. 45; Haskins, *Growth of English Representative Government*, 57.

bear the burden. The same tendency was probably even stronger in the cities, which were becoming centers for active trade in this period. The calling of knights and burgesses to parliament would aid the King in two ways. In the first place, he would get more revenue; and in the second, he would weaken the power of the magnates as his dependence upon them decreased. The contention that the representatives granted taxes in the reign of Edward I in return for redress of grievances seems to be based on a misapprehension.[38] The *Memoranda de Parliamento* shows that there were some common petitions presented to the King in his council in parliament, but these did not deal with complaints against royal officials. In the same manner that some historians tried to read the concept of "no taxation without representation" into the Great Charter, it seems that others are making a similar error in this case, of reading later ideas and practices into a period to which they were alien.[39] In our efforts to understand the place of Commons in the reign of Edward I, we can still do no better than Maitland and "fall back upon the words of the writ of summons; the commoners have been told to come in order that they may do what shall be ordained."[40]

It is impossible to draw a very firm distinction between the activity of the king in his council hearing petitions and its function as a court for civil and criminal suits. Professor McIlwain has spelled out specifically and in detail an essential concept of the "high court of Parliament."[41] We must divest ourselves of our modern notions of courts applying case law and statute law when thinking of the Parliament of Edward

[38] Pollard, *The Evolution of Parliament,* 54, 117.
[39] Haskins, "Petitions of Representatives in the Parliament of Edward I," *EHR,* Vol. LIII (1938), 19.
[40] "Introduction to *Memoranda de Parliamento,*" *Selected Essays,* 58.
[41] *The High Court of Parliament.*

I as essentially a court. In this sense it has been said that Edward "created the most effective law-declaring machine in the Teutonic world of his day."[42] This statement well illustrates the idea of the Anglo-Norman period that laws are declared and not made. The roots of this idea lie in the Anglo-Saxon *witan,* which had the authority to declare the law. When Duke William of Normandy became king of England, he declared that he had come not as a conqueror to change the law but as a rightful ruler to enforce the law of Edward the Confessor's day. Another important principle which can be derived from the central institutions of England of the early Middle Ages is the concept of a "fusion of indefinite powers."[43] In our efforts to apply the canons of historical objectivity scientifically, we must be careful not to give to a term a definite and rigid meaning which it did not have for those who used it.[44] The use of the word *"parliamentum"* by medieval chroniclers and clerks is a good illustration of the danger to which I refer. In his introduction to the *Memoranda de Parliamento,* Maitland summarized his conclusions about the nature of Parliament in the time of Edward I by stating that

> a session of the king's council is the core and essence of every *parliamentum,* that the documents usually called "parliamentary petitions" are petitions to the king and his council, that the auditors of petitions are committees of the council, that the rolls of parliament are the records of the business done by the council—sometimes with, but more often without, the concurrence of the estates of the realm—that the highest tribunal

[42] Edward Jenks, *Law and Politics in the Middle Ages,* 44.

[43] McIlwain, *The High Court of Parliament,* 119.

[44] William S. Holdsworth says, "If we look at one of our oldest printed Parliament Rolls—the roll of 1305—we shall see that large and vague words are needed to describe the facts."—*A History of English Law,* I, 352.

in England is not a general assembly of barons and prelates, but the king's council.[45]

The frequency and regularity of the parliaments of Edward I in conjunction with the development of the written petition determined the area in which the work of Parliament would lie.[46] There developed a tacit understanding that a petition presented to the King in his council in parliament would be answered before the end of the session. It is understood that the session did not necessarily end when the representative element departed, for its presence was not considered essential. Although this understanding was honored many times in the breach as well as in the observance, it endured until it became established. This would help to explain the appearance of an increasing number of petitions during the parliaments of Edward I.[47] Professor Plucknett takes issue with this principle because he has found at least two instances in which petitions have been presented to bodies which cannot justly be termed parliaments.[48] The real bone of contention here, however, is the definition of Parliament, not the answer-

[45] "Introduction to *Memoranda de Parliamento,*" *Selected Essays,* 70 f. Plucknett agrees: "In short, whether we examine parliament as a court or as an administrative body, it is for the most part only a reflection of the council, which exercised its powers in parliament, and was, in fact, the very core and heart of parliament."—"Parliament," in *The English Government at Work, 1327–1336,* I, 112. Holdsworth also accepts Maitland's definition of Parliament (*A History of English Law,* I, 352).

[46] Richardson and Sayles (eds.), *Rotuli Parliamentorum Anglie Hactenus Inediti MCCLXXIX–MCCCLXXIII, ix* f. "The petitioning of the king in his council in his parliament for remedy was undoubtedly one of the great formative influences behind the growth of the latter assembly; whilst the establishment of parliament as a body containing a wide-spread representation of the nation greatly extended the practice of petitions."—Bertie Wilkinson, *The Constitutional History of England, 1216–1399,* I, *Politics and the Constitution, 1216–1307,* 46.

[47] Richardson and Sayles, *Rotuli Parliamentorum, ix* f.

[48] "Parliament," in *The English Government at Work, 1327–1336,* 82–128.

43

ing of petitions. Since the real core of Parliament in this period is the king in his council, this essential element can do anything that Parliament can do and more in addition. For me this is a matter of semantics which illustrates my earlier statement regarding the indefiniteness of the institutions and ideas of the thirteenth century. It certainly does not vitiate the basic contention raised above. Although Plucknett's challenge has been in print for some years, apparently no one has, in writing at least, either agreed or disagreed with it, and Plucknett seems to have let it drop.

Although Maitland's Introduction to the *Memoranda de Parliamento of 1305* was published as early as 1893, it attracted little attention for nearly twenty years. Because Maitland's conclusions or observations were set forth in such a diffident manner and with so little fanfare on his part, no one seemed immediately to see the implications of his findings. It seems to me that scholars have read many of their own ideas and interpretations into Maitland's remarks. Maitland was not one to hide his lamp under a bushel. In other instances where he consciously presented a revisionary interpretation, he said so in plain words. For example, when he challenged the traditional concept of the law of the English church before the time of the Reformation, he boldly asserted his position and firmly substantiated it, even though his views were contrary to those of such a renowned scholar as Bishop Stubbs.

There is no question that other scholars have claimed to take Maitland's introduction as a point of departure. Referring to McIlwain, Baldwin, and himself, Pollard wrote: "The starting-point for all of us has been Maitland's introduction to the *Memoranda de Parliamento,* which he edited for the Rolls Series in 1893, the most original and suggestive essay that has ever been written on the medieval English parliament."[49] As I indicated earlier, it seems to me that recent scholars with a point of view different from that of Maitland have exaggerated the difference between the conclusions of Stubbs and Maitland in order to provide a transition between the nineteenth-century concept of the medieval parliament based upon a limited knowledge and modern concepts based upon a fuller knowledge. Maitland's views were expressed so simply and in such an unadorned manner that, like articles of a good constitution, they were subject to different interpretations. I can only conclude that either Maitland was not conscious of the implications of his remarks or else modern scholars have placed an interpretation upon those comments which Maitland himself would hardly recognize.

In conclusion, I find five principal views set forth by Maitland in this now famous introduction: (1) He understood a "full parliament" to mean the meeting of the king and his council with the three estates of the realm. (2) The king and his council were the essential elements in a Parliament. (3) Whatever else Parliament may have been, it was a court which could apparently exercise the functions of any of the central law courts. (4) The principal activity of Parliament was the trying or hearing of petitions. (5) Maitland understood that the purpose of the representative elements in Parliament was not to act on behalf of the realm, but to express the grievances of the country before the king in his council.

As has been said, Pollard completely discredited Maitland's view of a "full parliament" by showing that it was derived from a faulty translation of *in pleno parliamento*. Richardson and Sayles' research on the parliaments of both England and Ireland has served to emphasize Maitland's teaching "that, while parliament may have special functions, it is not *sui*

[49] *Evolution of Parliament, v* f.

generis but an afforced meeting of the king's council."[50] Professor George Haskins has noted that "the English parliament, like the *parlement* of Paris, was primarily a court set over other courts."[51] Charles McIlwain has said that the "most striking fact about the council in this feudal period was its varied functions. It was court of law, advisory council, and exchequer all in one."[52] Richardson and Sayles hold that when all the nonessential elements of Parliament have been removed (legislation, taxation, and representation), the essence which remains is "the dispensing of justice by the king or by someone who in a very special way represents the king." These two, who are undoubtedly the leading current authorities on this subject, agree with Maitland that "parliament is still, above all other times and places, the time and place for petitioning for favors or the remedying of wrongs."[53] To repeat, there are many who believe that the chief reason for the representatives of the shires and boroughs being summoned to meet the king in parliament was in order to approve taxes.

Although revisions have been made necessary by the increase in our knowledge of Parliament, there is still no reason to take exception to the last four of the five conclusions derived from Maitland's investigation. There is, however, one basic weakness, which Miss Cam has pointed out: "The nature of his record, which is far from giving a complete account of the Parliament of Easter, 1305, leads him to underestimate the unofficial or political aspects of a parliament."[54] It is to be regretted that Maitland did not take the occasion to examine

[50] *The Irish Parliament*, 8–9.
[51] *Growth of English Representative Government*, 22.
[52] *The High Court of Parliament*, 16.
[53] "Early Records of the English Parliament," *BIHR*, Vol. V (1931), 133, 71–72.
[54] Cam, in *Historical Essays*, xix.

the subject of parliament more fully. Shortly after Maitland's death, McIlwain, Baldwin, and Pollard did pick up his suggestions and elaborate them, though often with overemphasis. Some have complained that Maitland did not press his thesis more strongly and root out the misconceptions concerning Parliament which remained prevalent for some time. Yet, in the more than half a century since its publication, Maitland's provocative introduction to the *Memoranda de Parliamento* has served as an introduction to a more adequate understanding of the medieval parliament.

III

ORIGIN OF THE
COMMON LAW COURTS

MAITLAND HAS MADE TWO distinct contributions to our understanding of the development of a central system of courts for the administration of the common law of England. His exposition of this subject is found in three of his writings: *Select Pleas of the Crown,* his introduction to the *Parliamentary Roll of 1305,* and *The History of English Law.*[1] In each of the last three generations one scholar has stood out as the leading authority upon the common law courts of the thirteenth century. Although others have contributed to the subject, they all take their point of departure from one whom they recognize as being the chief authority upon the subject. In order to place the contributions of Maitland in their proper perspective, therefore, we must view the conclusions of his chief predecessor, William Stubbs, and those of George O. Sayles,[2] the chief writer of more recent days who has given to the study of the documents a diligent application at least equal to, if not actually surpassing, that of Maitland himself.

[1] *Select Pleas of the Crown, Vol. I, 1200–1225; Selected Essays, 61–70; History of English Law,* I, 153–83, 190–200.
[2] Stubbs, *The Constitutional History of England,* secs. 145, 163, and 233; Sayles, *The Court of King's Bench under Edward I.*

All agree that the king is the fount of justice, which in the eleventh and twelfth centuries is represented by the king and the *curia regis*. At this point unanimity ceases, for there is lack of harmony concerning the actual constitution of this body. In Chapter II above, attention was called to a controversy over whether or not a distinction should be made between the *curia regis* and the *magna curia regis*. Even those who disagree on this issue will concede that by some process the three common law courts—exchequer, common pleas, and king's bench—evolved from the *curia regis*. All jurisdiction not belonging to one of these courts remained in the hands of the *curia regis*, which tended, after the time of Edward I, to be more commonly referred to as the king's council, since it began to concern itself more largely with matters which we would call political rather than judicial.

The first line of division in the administration of royal justice can be drawn in the reign of Henry II between the permanent royal courts and those temporary courts which are specially commissioned from time to time to hear the pleas of the crown in particular counties. We find reference on the one hand to the *capitalis curia domini regis,* and on the other to *justitiarii itinerantes*.[3] During the reign of Henry, visitation of the counties by itinerant justices became systematic.

In 1166 the assize of Clarendon was enforced by a party of justices headed by Richard Lucy and Earl Geoffrey of Mandeville. In 1168 Richard of Ilchester, Guy the dean of Waltham, William Basset and Reginald Warenne visited most of the counties. In 1175 the north and east were perambulated by Ranulf Glanvill and Hugh of Cressi, the south and west by William of Lanvallei and Thomas Basset, while the king himself seems

[3] Introduction to *Select Pleas of the Crown*, xi.

to have been journeying with other justices in his suit. In 1176 to execute the assize of Northampton eighteen justices were employed and the country was divided into six circuits; in 1179 twenty-one justices were employed and the country was divided into four circuits; indeed from 1176 onwards hardly a year went by without there being a visitation of some part of England.[4]

Controversy first arose concerning the identity of the centralized royal court of justice which made its appearance toward the close of the twelfth century—was this the king's bench or the common bench? A contemporary chronicler, Benedict of Peterborough, tells us that when Henry II returned to England in July of 1178 after a sojourn of one year in Normandy, he heard complaints against the oppressive measures of the justices, of whom there was considered to be an excessive number. Without apparently dismissing these eighteen justices, the King, with the advice of his council, chose five of the members of his household, two clerks and three laymen, who, he decreed, should hear all complaints of the kingdom and do right in each case. These men should not depart from the king's court, but should reserve the more difficult cases to be decided by the King and the wiser men of the kingdom.[5]

Sir Edward Coke thought that the common bench came into existence in response to Chapter Seventeen of the Great Charter, which said that "common pleas shall not follow our court, but shall be held in some definite place."[6] This opinion was reaffirmed by Blackstone and acquiesced in, in the nine-

[4] Pollock and Maitland, *History of English Law*, I, 155 f.

[5] Benedict of Peterborough, *Gesta Regis Henrici Secundi Benedicti Abbatis*, ed. by William Stubbs, I, 207 f.

[6] Carl Stephenson and F. G. Marcham (trans. and eds.), *Sources of English Constitutional History: A Selection of Documents from A.D. 600 to the Present*, 118.

teenth century, by Hardy, Spence, Foss, Hallam, Gneist, and Stephen.[7] In the light of this general conception, it became necessary to conclude, with Stubbs, that the new court, established by order of the King in 1178, was the court of king's bench.[8] Stubbs' verdict was accepted without question by later writers until Maitland, in the first volume of the Selden Society Publications, propounded a revolutionary theory which necessitated a complete restatement of the accepted belief.[9]

Maitland made two distinct modifications in the accepted belief. For him, the group of men appointed to remain at Westminster to hear all pleas which should be brought to them was not the court of king's bench at all, but the court of common bench or court of common pleas. He further rejected the idea that this was a "new" court created as if by enactment. He preferred to place greater faith in the documents of the courts than in the wording of a chronicler, regardless of how well that chronicler may have understood the law. The two groups of justices represented for Maitland a division of the *curia regis*. We may recall that Maitland had rejected the distinction of a "great council." He based his contention on the fact that both bodies claimed to be the *curia regis* even in the most formal documents.[10]

Maitland then went on to the contention that the group of justices at Westminster divided during the early years of the reign of King John, with one group remaining at Westminster —the common bench—and the other group accompanying the King on his perambulations so long as he remained in England, returning to Westminster when he went abroad. This

[7] Sayles, *The Court of King's Bench*, I, xii f.
[8] *The Constitutional History of England*, sec. 145.
[9] *Select Pleas of the Crown*, xii ff.
[10] *Ibid.*, xii.

second court, which was not distinct either in the personnel of its justices or in the nature of the pleas which it heard, became known later as the king's bench. Its independent status was established beyond question from about 1234.

For Maitland, the earliest distinction between the court of king's bench and the court of common pleas is to be found in the wording of the writs which directed defendants to one or the other. He noted such a distinction as "appear before *our justices* at such or such a place," or "appear before *us* wheresoever we shall be in England." Among the pleas which Maitland published are several which illustrate this distinction, which suggests the existence of two definite courts in the time of King John. "The king tells the justices at Westminster to excuse A. B. for not having been before them on a certain day, because on that day he was *coram nobis in placito.*" It is difficult if not impossible to divide the plea rolls of the *capitalis curia* into two classes, *coram rege* rolls and *de banco* rolls, because the rolls are headed merely *"placita,"* followed by a date or *"placita apud Westmonasterium"* of such a date. Maitland came to the conclusion that although there were two distinct forms of summons during the reign of John and although the court could be in two places at one time, there were not two distinct courts. He gives four reasons in support of this conclusion: (1) Whenever the court is meeting in two places simultaneously each is equally competent to hear both common pleas and pleas of the crown. (2) There seems to be only one court whenever the King goes abroad. (3) Judges are not permanently assigned to either section, but seem to shuttle back and forth with no regularity. (4) Cases are transferred from one section to another at the will of the justices.[11]

By the time Henry III came to the throne, there were two

11 *Ibid., xiii* (italics are mine), *xiii* f., *xvi* f.

obvious changes. Article seventeen of the Great Charter had forbidden common pleas to follow the king, and, moreover, the King was now a minor incapable of holding pleas. About the time that Henry began to rule for himself, he began to travel about England as his predecessors had done, with justices in his train. These judges were constantly hearing cases. From about 1234 there are to be found two distinct sets of plea rolls, the *coram rege* and the *de banco* rolls.[12] For ordinary purposes, the court *coram rege* consisted of a few professional judges, but on special occasions its membership might be augmented by the presence of the king and his councillors.[13] On these occasions, the roll is entitled "Pleas before the king and his council," and it indicates that this body is able to correct errors from the court of common pleas.[14]

> Then early in Edward I's reign a further differentiation takes place. The court *coram rege* when it assumes its everyday shape—that of a tribunal consisting of a few professional justices—becomes "the king's bench"; what has formerly been "the bench," though it always preserves this title, becomes, in common parlance, "the common bench"; at a later day it will be the court of common pleas. But there is a greater change than this. A new set, unfortunately a meagre, disjointed set, of plea rolls (which, however, are not pure plea rolls, for they deal also with petitions and other matters) begins to appear. A court which is to stand above the king's bench is being evolved out of the old court held *coram rege;* its rolls are the "parliament rolls."[15]

It was at this point that Maitland advanced a theory which

[12] *Bracton's Note-Book,* I, 56–58.
[13] "Introduction to *Memoranda de Parliamento,*" *Selected Essays,* 62.
[14] *Bracton's Note-Book,* I, 56.
[15] "Introduction to *Memoranda de Parliamento,*" *Selected Essays,* 62 f.

has strongly influenced later writers on this subject. He was in-
timately acquainted with the writings of both Bracton and
Fleta.[16] In his study of Bracton, he found two sets of plea
rolls, while Fleta had to account for three. Bracton knew only
the court known as the bench (the court of common pleas)
and the court which accompanies the king's person.[17] In addition to these courts, Fleta knew the court of the king in his
council in his Parliament.[18] This new tribunal becomes the
highest court of the realm. It is the king in his council, but it
is also Parliament. To call this body a parliament goes against
the grain of our concepts of Parliament, which merely proves
that our concepts are not applicable to the thirteenth century.
This body dispenses extraordinary justice primarily. The dis-
tinguishing factor between ordinary and extraordinary justice
seems to be that the courts of the former keep a roll or record,
while the council does not.[19] To support his analysis, Maitland
pointed to the appearance of a third plea roll—*Rotuli Parliamentorum* which corresponded to the new court. "This conclusion has been accepted by most modern scholars (though
not by all) and widely applied."[20] This court, which is above
the king's bench, is a novelty in the time of Edward I. We
should probably say that in most cases its decisions were based
upon equity. It is dangerous to try to be too specific in describ-

---

[16] He edited *Bracton's Note-Book;* "Fleta," *DNB*, XIX, 290.

[17] *Bracton's Note-Book*, I, 56–58.

[18] Fleta: "Habet enim Rex curiam suam in consilio suo in parliamentis suis,
praesentibus praelatis, comitibus, baronibus, proceribus, et aliis viris peritis
ubi terminatae sunt dubitationes judiciarum et novis injuriis emersis nova con-
stituuntur remedia, et unicuique justitia prout meruit retribuetur ibidem."
Cited by Maitland in "Introduction to *Memoranda de Parliamento*," *Selected
Essays*, 64, n. 1.

[19] "Introduction to *Memoranda de Parliamento*," *Selected Essays*, 65.

[20] Plucknett, "Parliament," in *The English Government at Work, 1327-1336*,
I, 90.

ing or defining the powers of a newly evolved institution. This court is not primarily a court of appeal but a court of first instance, and, as Fleta tells us, "judicial doubts are determined and new remedies established for new wrongs." Thus we have returned to the judicial business of Parliament which we deferred from the last chapter.

Knowing as we do that in the fourteenth century the king in his council in his Parliament will evolve into the nascent House of Lords, it is likely that we will anticipate problems which may not have actually existed in the thirteenth century. In the time of Edward I there need not have been mutual antipathy and jealousy between the aristocratic councillors and the professional lawyers and judges. So long as the King neither imposed new taxes nor issued new statutes without their consent, the barons probably hoped that he would confine himself to governing the realm and leave them alone.[21] It is not likely that many magnates in the time of Edward I were interested in making a long, costly trip at their own expense in order to listen to pleas in which they had neither interest nor concern, merely for the satisfaction of wielding political power. Although no exact time can be given when the jurisdiction of the king's council ended and that of the House of Lords began, we do know that one important factor in this transition was the cessation of voting by the judges.[22]

In 1894, L. O. Pike, in his *Constitutional History of the House of Lords,* elaborated the explanation which Maitland had given of the significance of Henry II's action in 1178.[23] Although he did not refer to the writings of Maitland, he added new evidence to bolster the interpretation Maitland

---

[21] "Introduction to *Memoranda de Parliamento,*" *Selected Essays,* 70.
[22] McIlwain, *The High Court of Parliament,* 32 f.
[23] *The Constitutional History of the House of Lords,* 33-34.

had suggested.[24] Only one person seems to have taken exception to the views expressed by Maitland regarding the common bench. Although many have crossed swords with Maitland's views on the king's bench, George Burton Adams is the only one to push the dispute back to the origin of the court of common bench. His motive primarily seems to have been to give a stronger foundation for his later challenge to Maitland's position on the origin of the king's bench.[25]

For the first point in his case, Adams recites the Latin text of the chronicler's account of the King's action. He then goes on to tell us that the chronicler "had a knowledge of institutional matters unusual in a chronicler, and his technical language is, I think, everywhere accurate." The creation of the court of common bench was a "deliberate legislative act" on the part of the king in his council to supplement loopholes which became apparent in the system of itinerant justices instituted two years earlier.[26] According to Adams, this court was not formed, as Maitland had suggested, by a mere division of the *curia regis*. Adams believed that his own interpretation of the origin of the common bench was apparent in its development or lack of it. Although the procedure in the court develops as the amount of business increases rapidly, the "court

[24] Holdsworth, *The History of English Law*, I, 195 ff.; Reginald Lane Poole, *The Exchequer in the Twelfth Century*, 180, 182; W. S. McKechnie, *Magna Carta*, 263; Sayles, *The Court of King's Bench*, xiii.

[25] George Burton Adams, *Councils and Courts in Anglo-Norman England;* and *The Origin of the English Constitution*, 136–43.

[26] Adams, *Origin of the English Constitution*, 136, 736 f. Sayles points out, "Whilst in no way wishing to underrate the value of this passage, we are not disposed to overemphasize it: it is too unique and isolated evidence. . . . We know with certainty that three years earlier than the ordinance in 1178 a group of justices had attended the king as he travelled through the country north of the Thames and held pleas in *curia regis*, nor are they identifiable as justices in eyre."—*The Court of King's Bench*, I, xx f. This latter evidence in no way weakens Maitland's case, but seems difficult to reconcile with a "deliberate legislative act."

institutionally considered remains to the end what it was at the beginning."[27] In the thirteenth century, a clear line of distinction develops between the court of common pleas on one side and the other two common law courts (*coram rege* and exchequer[28]), which continue the functions of the council of which they are the natural outgrowth. This contention is based upon the premise that the common bench was from the very beginning the court of "common pleas," for "there is nothing to imply any intention to employ this court in king's pleas."[29] Both Maitland, who studied the plea rolls of John's reign, and Mr. C. T. Flower, who edited them, do not find evidence for the distinction which Adams makes.

Most later writers have continued to follow Maitland and to reject Adams' contention. Baldwin is the only historian, to my knowledge, who has accepted Adams' view.[30] Holdsworth, in his *History of English Law,* follows Maitland in explaining the origin of the court of common pleas.[31] Referring to Adams' statement specifically, in a note he rejects his explanation. The first volume of the *curia regis* rolls of the reigns of Richard I and John, published in 1922, contains distinct rolls for the second year of John's rule. One set recorded pleas which were plainly tried *coram rege* as the term was then used, and the other set, pleas which were with equal certainty tried at Westminster. In commenting upon this fact, Mr. Flower said of the first of these rolls, in accordance with Maitland's suggestion, "It is therefore probable . . . that the roll now under

---

[27] Adams, *Councils and Courts,* 227.

[28] It should be mentioned that Maitland did not find an occasion or perhaps the necessity for discussing the third of the common law courts—the exchequer.

[29] Adams, *Councils and Courts,* 224; *ibid., Origin of the English Constitution,* 137.

[30] *The King's Council,* 47.

[31] I, 51 f.

consideration is an example of the bifurcation of the legal business of the court in *placita coram rege* and *placita de banco.*"[32] Professor F. M. Powicke, in reviewing this work, stated: "The most striking fact which can be deduced from the rolls of John published by Mr. Flower is that, long before the time when Henry III began to hold pleas in person and the two series of plea rolls regularly appear (1234), the cases which came before the king were recorded on a separate roll."[33]

Although Maitland's writings did not remove the king's bench from the arena of conflict, opinion has in general tended to follow his conclusions, modifying his statements in the light of the more recently published *curia regis* rolls. The problem was no longer that of confusion with the court of common pleas but over the time and the process by which it became separated from the king's council.[34] There has been a tendency to postpone the establishment of a distinct and readily identifiable court of king's bench on the grounds that "the substantial identity of the court known as *coram rege* and the council is abundantly shown in the plea rolls themselves." It is contended that in the plea rolls there is not the distinction between cases that we would call conciliar and those that would be called *coram rege* cases; therefore, "during the reign of Edward I the king's bench was not fully a court of common law."[35] Another has found that "under Edward I the king's bench was not yet quite distinct from the council."[36] This line of thought reaches its extreme position in the writings of Adams. For him, the judges who traveled with King John were simply a duplicate of the court sitting at

[32] *Curia Regis Rolls,* I, 254 n. 1.
[33] *EHR,* Vol. XXXIX (1924), 265.
[34] Sayles, *The Court of King's Bench,* I, xiv.
[35] Baldwin, *The King's Council,* 54, 209.
[36] D. Pasquet, *Essay on the Origins of the House of Commons,* 7.

Westminster—a court of common pleas which was to vanish after Magna Carta forbade common pleas to follow the king. Thereafter, *coram rege* in a technical sense comes to mean the "council acting in its judicial capacity," and it was not until after the Barons' Wars that contemporaries could recognize the existence of an independent court of king's bench.[37]

The most recent authoritative attempt to refine our knowledge of the court of king's bench is to be found in the introduction to *Select Cases in the Court of King's Bench under Edward I,* by George O. Sayles, who spent three or four months a year for fifteen years at the Public Record Office engaged in this enterprise. He suggests that there are two basic questions which no one has attempted to answer: what judges sat in the court of king's bench before the death of Henry III and at what time and for what reasons this court tended to confine its main attention to felonies and trespasses.[38] These questions only become relevant in the light of the work which Maitland did on the origin of this body.

The fairly continuous series of plea rolls attests to the existence of two courts since 1234. No serious attempt to separate personnel of the two courts has been made, but as Maitland tersely put it, one man cannot be in two places at the same time. So extreme has been the desire to prove a late origin for the court of king's bench that one writer has contended that the court *coram rege* under John was a duplicate court of common pleas and that the court *coram rege* under Henry III was the council.[39] Yet it is plain that the line of connection between them is unbroken, as Maitland originally contended. When Henry went abroad in 1242–43 and 1253–54, there

[37] Adams, *Councils and Courts,* 206, 230 f., 241.
[38] I, *xv, xxv.*
[39] Adams, *Councils and Courts.*

could be no court in England which was actually *coram rege,* though the court which bears that title moved to Westminster and continued to function rather than disappear, as it had done when John went abroad. The pleas were said to come before the council and not before the King, but as soon as the King returned home, the expression *coram rege* reappeared with him. Sayles noted this convention during the absence of "Edward I, when the fact of a distinct court of king's bench is beyond dispute."[40]

Let us now summarize the principal conclusions which Maitland drew concerning the origin of the central law courts. We have noted that Maitland did not discuss the court of the exchequer. The court of common pleas, he maintained, resulted from the division of the *curia regis* during the reign of Henry II, probably about the year 1178. This court was not created, as George Burton Adams declared, by a legislative act which excluded from its jurisdiction pleas of the crown. It was noted above that Adams' contention rests merely on the wording of a chronicler. Luke Pike, in an independent investigation of the origin of the court of common pleas, has come to the same conclusion arrived at by Maitland:

> It will be observed that the five Justices of the King's court appointed at this time (1178) are not said to have any authority in crown matters. They are only to hear the claims or plaints of parties, and not even to determine the plaints if any special questions should arise. Here to all appearance, the court of common pleas comes into being.[41]

In other words, the only limitation of this court seems to have been that difficult cases or cases in which the King had

[40] Sayles, The *Court of King's Bench,* I, xxvii.
[41] *Constitutional History of the House of Lords,* 32.

a personal interest should be tried in his presence. Sayles points out that "Maitland's views as regards the common bench have been endorsed by all later writers."[42]

Maitland found that the court *coram rege* resulted from a division of the court of common pleas prior to 1234, since from this time on, two distinct sets of plea rolls were kept. He further suggested that this separation probably began during the early years of the reign of King John. This, however, is purely a matter of interpretation if not speculation, because it rests not upon the wording of the writs but upon inference drawn from them. Here again Adams differs with Maitland since he believed that the establishment of these two courts was interrelated. Adams, in rejecting Maitland's interpretation, followed the older view which confused the king's bench with the common bench. Once more I must accept the decision of Sayles, who devoted fifteen years to the study of the court of king's bench, when he declared that "opinion has in general been inclined to follow Maitland, modifying his statements slightly, in the light of the newly-published Curia Regis Rolls."[43] These rolls suggest that the court of king's bench may have originated even earlier than Maitland suggested. Certainly those who postulate a later date for the origin of the court *coram rege*[44] stand on less firm ground than does Maitland.

Even after the establishment of these two distinct courts, there was no doubt, for Maitland, that in the reign of Edward I the fount of justice and the highest court in the land was the king in his council in his Parliament.

[42] *The Court of King's Bench,* I, *xiii.*
[43] *Ibid.*
[44] Baldwin, *The King's Council;* A. B. White, *The Making of the English Constitution, 449–1485,* 178, 179 n.; Pasquet, *Origins of the House of Commons,* 7; and Adams, *Councils and Courts,* chaps. VIII and X, especially pp. 206, 229, 241.

IV

CANON LAW
IN ENGLAND

MAITLAND WAS ATTRACTED to the subject of English canon law through writing the *History of English Law*. He had become involved in deciphering the law with regard to marriage. It soon became apparent that it would be necessary to investigate, from the documents as was Maitland's wont, the basis for the law with regard to the institution of marriage. As he pored over the records of the council meetings of the English ecclesiastics and the decretals and codes of the pope and the Roman Catholic church, Maitland became conscious that the evidence before him did not harmonize with the accepted doctrines with regard to the development of the English church. He turned for confirmation of his hypotheses to the Report of the Ecclesiastical Courts Commission.[1] Bishop Stubbs had summarized the accepted doctrines with regard to the English church in a historical introduction to this report. Realizing that if Stubbs was not aware of what the sources contained on the canon law of the English church, probably no one was, Maitland sought to find out the truth of the matter. He was one of the first scholars to become interested in the

[1] Vol. I (1883).

history of law for its own sake rather than as a mere adjunct to some other dominant concern. It must be stated at the outset that what Maitland accomplished in this area was more in the nature of filling a lacuna than in making a basic revision founded upon well-known evidence. It was without apparent embarrassment that the great Bishop was forced to admit that Maitland's conclusions appeared far more valid than those which they displaced.[2] Maitland's case is so sound and so well substantiated that it stands today without controversy. His work was so basic that it opened a whole new field of study which other scholars have for the past half-century been exploring and explaining.

In the Report of the Ecclesiastical Courts Commission referred to above, Maitland found a statement which served as the central theme for his book on *Roman Canon Law in the Church of England.* "But the canon law of Rome, although always regarded as of great authority in England, was not held to be binding on the courts."[3] Maitland understood that "the courts" referred to the ecclesiastical courts of England in the three centuries before the Reformation. Obviously this is the meaning which the authors had intended, and Maitland's interpretation has not been challenged or criticized as being polemic. Maitland concluded that although the statement quoted above was carefully worded, it "is questionable and should be questioned."[4] He was not one to shirk an obvious task.

Before Maitland's investigation, the English ecclesiastical courts were understood to manifest for " 'the canon law of Rome' the respect which nowadays an English Court will pay

[2] McIlwain, *The High Court of Parliament,* 13, n. 4.
[3] Ecclesiastical Courts Commission, 1883, I, *xviii,* quoted by Maitland in *Canon Law,* 2.
[4] *Canon Law,* 2.

to an American or an Irish decision."[5] Roman canon law was not regarded as statute law by the English ecclesiastical courts, for the English church could exercise its prerogative in determining which part of the Roman law it would "accept" as applicable within the ecclesiastical courts of England. The papal law-books were regarded merely as manuals, but not as codes of statutes. It was generally believed that attempts to force on the "church" and nation the complete canon law of the Middle Ages were unsuccessful. Neither proof nor illustration was forthcoming in support of this position:

> The laws which guided the English courts up to the time of the Reformation may, then, be thus arranged: (1) the canon law of Rome, comprising the decretum of Gratian; the decretals of Gregory IX., published in 1230; the Sext, added by Boniface VIII.; the Clementines, issued in 1318; and the Extravagants, or uncodified edicts, of the succeeding popes. A knowledge of these was the scientific equipment of the ecclesiastical jurist, but the texts were not authoritative.[6]

Maitland disagreed with the assertion that these texts "were not authoritative." The Report goes on to state that at the Council of Merton, the King and the English barons refused to permit the national law of marriage to be modified by these papal texts; therefore the papal texts were to have no force in England when they opposed the laws of England.[7] Although this incident does not support the principle raised above, it is implied in the Report that no more need be said on this subject. Maitland, however, ably defended the position that

---

[5] *Ibid.*
[6] Ecclesiastical Courts Commission, 1883, I, 23, quoted by Maitland in *Canon Law*, 52.
[7] *Ibid.*, 53.

A Page from Bracton's Law-Book

HENRY III, KING OF ENGLAND 1216–72

EDWARD I, KING OF ENGLAND 1272–1307

at least some parts, and in all probability large portions, of the "canon law of Rome" were regarded by the "courts Christian" in England "as absolutely binding statute law."[8]

It seems apparent that the ideas with regard to the law of the English church prevalent when Maitland wrote were "born" in the seventeenth century, long after the separation of the Church of England from that of Rome. In part at least, the acceptance of these ideas was probably motivated by an attempt to justify an act which was part of the heritage of the Anglican church and in addition was based upon a nascent national pride. It was undoubtedly the latter which was responsible for harboring and fostering this false notion in the nineteenth century. Few English historians seemed to have had the polemic spirit which causes one to go around looking for skeletons in closets which might be exposed. Perhaps it is putting it too strongly to imply that Maitland had a polemic spirit, but there is no doubt that when he thought he saw a historical truth, he hewed to the line and let the chips fall where they might.

We must now follow Maitland as he constructs a case for his interpretation:

> Now the principal witness whom we have to examine if we would discover the theory of law which prevailed in our English ecclesiastical courts about a hundred years before the breach with Rome, is indubitably William Lyndwood. He finished his gloss on the provincial constitutions of the archbishops of Canterbury in the year 1430. When he was engaged on this task he was the archbishop's principal official: in other words, his position made him the first man in England whose opinion we should wish to have about any question touching the nature of the ecclesiastical law that was being administered in England.[9]

[8] *Canon Law*, 2.   [9] *Ibid.*

Lyndwood had become little more than a name by the time Maitland began to examine his life and writings in the interests of clarifying the nature of canon law in England before the separation from Rome under Henry VIII. The "early date at which his book was first printed and the subsequent editions of it are a testimony to the high repute in which it stood before the Reformation."[10] For his day, Lyndwood must be considered both learned and able. He seemed to be well read in modern books of both Italian and French canonists, although he did often cite older works secondhand. Maitland anticipated the criticism that his "witness" could not be accepted as being typical because he was so learned and able as to make him outstanding in his own day. In reply to this possible charge, Maitland countered with the contention that Lyndwood in discussing canon law would be most apt to "state the law that he administered in the chief of all the English ecclesiastical courts."[11]

As an even earlier witness than Lyndwood, Maitland cited John of Ayton, the glossator of the *Legatine Constitutions*. He wrote his gloss between 1333 and 1348 while John of Stratford was archbishop of Canterbury and he himself was a canon of Lincoln. Maitland could find no evidence that either John of Ayton or Lyndwood ever denied, disputed, or even debated the binding force of any decretal: "I have looked in vain for any suggestion that an English judge or advocate ever called in question the statutory power of a text that was contained in any of the three papal law-books,"[12] With the publication of the Clementines in 1317, the age of great papal legislation came to an end. The "extravagants" which were issued after

[10] *Ibid.*, 4 f. Maitland used the Oxford edition of 1679, in which the *Provinciale* is followed by the *Legatine Constitutions* with John of Ayton's gloss.
[11] *Ibid.*, 5.
[12] *Ibid.*, 6, 9. The Decretals, the Sext, and the Clementines.

this time dealt with few topics and seldom gave rise to litigation in English courts. Lyndwood had little to do with "extravagant" constitutions; but if he did touch upon any, he cited them as law.[13] Maitland gave one illustration from Lyndwood which revealed the "difficulties besetting any theory which would ascribe 'great authority' but no binding power to papal ordinances." The *Vas Electionis* enacts a tariff expressly for England among other countries. The pope said that an English prelate on the occasion of a visitation should not receive more than a certain amount of money. A statute of this nature must either be obeyed or broken. For Lyndwood it was law. He admitted that in England custom in many cases determined the amount that the "archidiaconal" visitor was to receive, but in all other cases not covered by this custom the *Vas Electionis* was to prevail.[14]

It was necessary for Lyndwood to gloss and comment upon various ambiguous phrases in the three principal papal lawbooks. Although there was an opportunity for controversy and interpretation in the *Provinciale,* Lyndwood did not give any evidence of doubting the pope's legislative power or the validity of his decretals. John of Ayton is even more extreme in his support of papal authority in England. In a discussion of the *dominium* of the pope, John cited *Unam Sanctam,* that extreme bull of Boniface VIII, in which is asserted not only the spiritual but also the temporal supremacy of the pope.[15] John could hardly have believed that he had freedom to pick

[13] *Ibid.,* 10. "A decretum, says Lyndwood, is what the pope has ordained with the counsel of his cardinals when no one has consulted him; a decretal is what the pope either with or without the cardinals has ordained when anyone has consulted him. There is to be no picking and choosing, decretals are laws."—*Ibid.,* 18.

[14] *Ibid.,* 10.

[15] *Ibid.,* 11, 14.

and choose among the decretals, or he almost certainly would not have referred to this decretal, which even later popes felt had gone too far.

Maitland pointed out the apparent absence of any tradition of "Anglican independence" among the canonists of Lyndwood's day. Although Lyndwood was writing a textbook for beginners, it is difficult to see how, in the days between the councils of Constance and Basel, he could have "hurried past the momentous controversy of the age with a hint, or more than a hint, that the papal was the better opinion," if he held even mildly to a tradition of "Anglican independence." But Lyndwood leaves no one in doubt concerning his real opinion —the pope is the *princeps* of the church: *Quod principi placuit legis habet vigorem.*[16] The pope is above the law. Any general constitution made by the pope is binding two months after its publication, even on those who are ignorant of it. The decretals stand on a level with the canons of councils. To dispute the authority of a decretal is to be guilty of heresy at a time when obstinate heresy is a capital crime.[17]

This last is no private opinion of a glossator; it is a principle to which the archbishop, bishops, and clergy of the province of Canterbury have adhered by solemn words. Anyone who

---

[16] *Ibid.*, 15, 16; Lyndwood, 28.

[17] Lyndwood, 321: "Et hoc veram praeterquam in papa qui non subiacet legibus, ff. de legi. 1 princeps (Dig. I 3. 31)."—Maitland, *Canon Law,* 17; Lyndwood, 51: "Constitutio vero papae generallis post duos menses computandos a tempore publicationis eiusdem generaliter factae in consistorio legat etiam ignorantes."—*Ibid.,* 17. Lyndwood, 297: "Et nota quod decretales summorum pontificum sunt eiusdem auctoritatis sicut decreta quae sunt in corpore canonum digesta, 19 Dist. quase per totum. Parificantur etiam canonibus conciliorum. 20 Dist. per totum."—*Ibid.,* 17 Lyndwood, 292: "Dicitur etiam haereticus qui ex contemptu Romanae ecclesiae contemnit servare ea quae Romana ecclesia statuit, et etiam qui despicit et negligit servare decretales . . . ."—*Ibid.,* 17.

calls in question the authority of a decretum, is a heretic, and unless he will recant and abjure, must be burnt alive.[18]

It has seemed desirable to let the reader see for himself at least part of the solid base upon which Maitland rested his substantial judgment that Roman canon law and English canon law were nearly indistinguishable a century before the appearance of two distinct churches. The church law that Lyndwood administered in his court could have had only slight foundation in English customs and even then an advocate would find it necessary to produce proof that some words of Innocentius or Hostiensis or Johannes Andreae expressly left room for such a custom.[19]

Lyndwood made no use of any English "case law," any "case law" of English ecclesiastical courts.[20] There is no indication in his glosses that he was even an Englishman. Certainly the decisions of his English predecessors were not to be compared with the judgments of the Sext or the Clementines. This is more significant when one considers the strides which were being made in English temporal law. The Year Books were appearing regularly, and the most thoroughly national system of temporal law in Western Europe was emerging. Although the English state was an independent unit, the English church was only a fragment of the universal Christian church and abided by the laws which were imposed from without. This does not mean that there was no English canon law, for there was. It was necessary to extend the knowledge of some sections of the *corpus,* to repeat passages from the papal law-books, and to apply the general principles to the local conditions.

[18] *Canon Law,* 17.
[19] *Ibid.,* 42.
[20] *Ibid.,* 44.

Local laws were issued by national, legatine, and provincial synods, which primarily completed and glossed rather than repeated the law of the *corpus iuris*.[21] An English synod meeting at Oxford in 1222 added to the Lateran decree on vicarages a fixed minimum salary for vicars, and declared that Jews should wear a piece of cloth on their garments which would distinguish them from Christians.[22] It is necessary to note the inferiority of the local law to the common law of the church. The laws glossed by John of Ayton and William Lyndwood declared in England the universal law of the church, and in some respects developed and modified it.

Maitland has shown that anyone who would insist that the English ecclesiastical courts were developing their own system of laws and exercising the liberty of choosing the laws embodied in *corpore Decretorum et Decrelalium* must reject Lyndwood as an exception, for he is certainly a papalist who would abide neither custom nor liberty which could be raised against the law-giving power of the pope.[23] Maitland has cast the burden of proof upon those who think they see independent ecclesiastical courts in England which are not bound by the three papal law-books. No one even thought of bearing the burden of this proof before Maitland, and all further study since then has shown that it could not be borne.[24]

21 Professor Z. N. Brooke has demonstrated the papalism of twelfth-century English church law in "The Effects of Becket's Murder on Papal Authority in England," *CHJ*, Vol. II (1927), and *The English Church and the Papacy*. Miss Jane Lang has shown how episcopal administration in the time of Henry III was molded by the Fourth Lateran decrees (Marion Gibbs and Jane Lang, *Bishops and Reform, 1215–1272*, part iii: "The Reform Work of the Episcopate on the Lines Laid Down by the Lateran Council of 1215").

22 C. R. Cheney, "Legislation of the Medieval English Church," *EHR*, Vol. L (1935), 202–203.

23 *Canon Law*, 47.

24 C. R. Cheney, "Legislation of the Medieval English Church," *EHR*, Vol. L (1935), 194.

The misunderstanding on this subject seems in large part to have resulted from a related issue. In England it was generally and correctly understood that the state did not permit the church to exercise jurisdiction over so wide a field as was claimed by the clergy as the proper domain of ecclesiastical law. As a result of the fact that the ecclesiastical courts in England did not exercise all of the jurisdiction claimed by Roman canon law, it has too often been assumed that the English church rejected those portions of the Roman canon law that it did not exercise. This was not true at all, for in most of these cases the king of England refused to permit the clergymen of England who held land from him to exercise a jurisdiction to which he was personally opposed. Maitland strongly implies that the times and the issues upon which the English church courts departed from the canon law of Rome were those in which the secular courts were aggressively asserting their authority.[25] He illustrates this point by referring to the conflict between secular and church courts over the legitimization of children born to people who have co-habited without benefit of clergy. The church ruled that the marriage of the couple made all of their children legitimate, whereas the king's court held that the children remained bastards. Temporal courts, in seeking to enforce their ruling, asked clergymen to state specifically whether or not a child was born before the marriage of his parents. It is to be understood that this was a matter of church record, for no civil records of this nature were maintained. The bishops, not willing to give aid in enforcing a matter which went against canon law, refused. The state, however, was able to gain the information from a

[25] "Is it not even possible that the submissiveness of the ecclesiastical courts to the canon law of Rome varied directly rather than inversely with the strength and aggressiveness of their secular rivals?"—*Canon Law*, 52.

jury of the neighbors of the individuals in question. For the church it was a constant source of humiliation that the king's court refused to make the canonical test of legitimacy the basis for the English law of inheritance, and the judges of the church courts were tempted to try to interfere with the question of the right to the lay fief.[26] Maitland concluded that in this controversy the "honors were divided, but the state, as by this time its habit was, took the odd trick."[27]

The leaders of the church in England had to endure much that was contrary to the canon law of the church. The necessity of their yielding to secular force was more than a matter of mere expediency. Popes, in dealing with temporal power, had set an example of "temporizing." The concession or conclusion which we have reached on this point does not mean that merely because the bishops did not vigorously protest against the exercise, by secular courts, of jurisdiction claimed by canon law, they were either neglecting their duty or creating an "Anglican canon law which differs from the Roman.[28]

The conflict between church and state to which we have referred came to a climax in the reign of Henry II. Maitland could not examine the general question of canon law in England without letting his incisive mind come to rest upon this much debated topic. He tells us, "I have no wish to make myself a judge between the king and the archbishop, or between Freeman and Froude."[29] There seemed to Maitland to be a difference of opinion about a fact as well as about interpretation. It was this controversial "fact" to which he addressed himself. Perhaps we should indicate at the outset that

26 Mary Cheney, "The Compromise of Avranches," *EHR*, Vol. LVI (1941), 188 f.

27 *Canon Law*, 53 f.

28 *Ibid.*, 57.

29 *Ibid.*, 132.

the summary of Maitland's position as found in *The History of English Law*[30] is still the accepted view.[31]

What did Henry II propose to do with a cleric who was accused of a crime? Maitland revealed that it was possible to place two different interpretations upon the famous clause of the Constitutions of Clarendon which dealt with criminous clerics by offering an alternative to the one which held the field at the time that he wrote.[32] Before looking at the interpretations, we should have the clause before us:

> Clerici retati et accusati de quacunque re, summoniti a Justitia regis veniant in curiam ipsius, responsuri ibidem de hoc unde videbitur curiae regis quod ibidem sit respondendum; et in curia ecclesiastica, unde videbitur quod ibidem sit respondendum; ita quod Justitia regis mittet in curiam sanctae ecclesiae ad videndum qua ratione res ibi tractabitur. Et si clericus convictus vel confessus fuerit, non debet de cetero eum ecclesia tueri.[33]

According to the interpretation of this clause which was commonly accepted before Maitland expressed his views, crimes for which a cleric might be tried were either temporal or ecclesiastical. Murder, robbery, larceny, rape, and similar offenses were temporal, while heresy, incontinence, disobedience to superiors, breach of ceremonial rules, and the like were ecclesiastical. For a temporal offense, a cleric must stand trial in the king's court as any layman would; whereas, for an ecclesiastical offense, he would be tried in a church court. The King,

[30] (2d ed.) I, 447–57.

[31] Stephenson and Marcham, *Sources of English Constitutional History*, 74, n. 1.

[32] *Canon Law*, 132–47; "Canon Law in England," *EHR*, Vol. XI (1896), 446–78, 641–72.

[33] William Stubbs, *Select Charters* (9th ed.), 164 f.

however, decided which offenses were temporal and which were ecclesiastical; moreover, he demanded the right to send his representatives to view the proceedings in the spiritual tribunals. This traditional interpretation leaves several questions unanswered. Why should Henry be concerned over the activity of the ecclesiastical courts if their jurisdiction is purely with violations of church law? The last words of this clause said that if the clergyman is convicted or confesses, the church should no longer protect him. Maitland asks, "Has been convicted of what? Has confessed what? Some temporal crime it must be."[34]

Maitland presented his rival interpretation. He contended that the author of the clause in question was not thinking of two classes of offenses. For purely ecclesiastical offenses a man would be tried and punished by a spiritual court. A clerk who was accused of a serious crime should be summoned before the king's court to answer there *(respondere)* for what he ought to answer for—namely breach of the king's peace. If he confessed or admitted the crime of which he was accused, he should be unfrocked by the church for breaking the canon law and be punished by the royal officials. It should go without saying that all serious crimes were offenses in the eyes of canon law. If the accused came and "defended the breach of the king's peace word by word," he should, without a trial, be turned over to the ecclesiastical court for trial. If the spiritual court convicted him, it would unfrock him and turn him over to the royal authorities. The presence of the royal officials in the ecclesiastical court was to prevent the escape of the suspect in case he should be convicted. He would then be returned to the king's court, now no longer a member of the clergy, but a layman, and should be sentenced and punished.[35]

[34] *Canon Law*, 134.

Not only did this explanation seem more reasonable and probable to Maitland in the light of surrounding circumstances, but he was able to find three contemporary expositions to substantiate his interpretation. After marshaling the evidence in support of his contention, Maitland concluded, "Testimony that could be put into the other scale I cannot find."[36] Although Maitland was able to present evidence in support of his contention, the real strength of his position seems to rest primarily upon the force which the logic of his argument possesses. As was suggested earlier, Maitland's unique interpretation has weathered more than half a century and yet still stands untarnished.[37]

Now that we have Henry's scheme clearly in mind, let us see how Maitland explained its relationship to the law of the Catholic church in the year 1164. It is certain that Becket objected to the whole arrangement in the name of the church. There are two specific points at which those who took their stand on the Decretum must dissent. A cleric in orders certainly should not be accused before a temporal court, while the presence of the king's officers in the church court was a direct affront to ecclesiastical justice. This was not the principal issue, however, in the debate between the King and the Archbishop. Becket propounded a doctrine of double punishment in the name of the church which had not been "consecrated by the church." He contended that the state should not punish a criminous cleric who had already been unfrocked for his crime. This position has not been maintained by

[35] Maitland's account can be found in three places: *Canon Law*, 52 ff.; *History of English Law*, I, 447–57; and "Canon Law in England," *EHR* Vol. XI (1896), 446–78, 641–72.

[36] *Canon Law*, 136–39.

[37] "For the best interpretation, see Pollock and Maitland, I, 447 f."– Stephenson and Marcham, *Sources of English Constitutional History*, 74, n. 4.

masters of the canon law and was specifically repudiated by Innocent III.[38] Henry had no "hope of securing the consent of the English bishops to a treatment of accused clerks which was unquestionably condemned by the Decretum."[39]

In both England and France, the royal courts actively and successfully resisted what they considered to be encroachments of the church. The church claimed jurisdiction over matters of an ecclesiastical or spiritual nature and over causes in which at least some of the litigants were specially subject to the ecclesiastical jurisdiction.[40] Maitland pointed out that in England, particularly from Henry II's time onward, the temporal power by means of "writs of prohibition" kept for itself all litigation about advowsons.[41] Neither Henry nor Becket was fully aware of the significance of the question that was at stake, "for they could not foresee the limitless claims over all ecclesiastical preferments that were to be made by the popes of a later age." Henry's assertion that advowsons were outside the scope of ecclesiastical courts was the foundation for all subsequent legislation against "provisors." "The advowson is temporal property; the laws of the church and the courts of the church cannot touch it." The king's justices administered royal law not canon law when dealing with matters over which the church claimed jurisdiction. Therefore, when advowson was successfully assumed by the royal court, it became subject to temporal law.[42] Glanvill's chapter on advowsons implied that the king's court was successful in enforcing its claims; nevertheless, "No concession was made [by the church] to the theory on which the claim of the secular authority was based."[43] By Bracton's day

[38] *History of English Law*, I, 454, 455.
[39] *Canon Law*, 147.
[40] *History of English Law*, I, 125.
[41] "Canon Law in England," *Collected Papers*, III, 76.
[42] *Canon Law*, 63, 76.

a large number of rules had grown up around the subject of advowson; indeed, Maitland suggests that about no other subject does Bracton cite so many precedents.[44]

The arrangement whereby the parish priest was instituted by the bishop, although chosen by the landowner, seems to have originated as a compromise between the demand for control over the lower clergy by the church and the strong sense of possession on the part of the patron, whose ancestors had built the church, and who naturally therefore was interested in the choice of the priest who would serve his family and village.[45] "Henry II maintained, Becket controverted, Alexander condemned this principle; but despite papal condemnation, it seems to have been steadily upheld by the king's court," which maintained the right of patronage against the claims of the church courts.[46] Maitland's conclusion upon this subject is currently being cited as the "accepted view."[47]

By the end of the thirteenth century, the church in England, Maitland observed, had been particularly successful at two points:

> In the first place, the sentence of excommunication, when pronounced by the ecclesiastical courts, was enforced by the secular power with mechanical regularity and almost as a matter of course. The excommunicate was disabled from suing in the temporal courts: the contumacious excommunicate was thrown into gaol. In the second place, the canonists had acquired what

[43] Mary Cheney, "The Compromise of Avranches," *EHR*, Vol. LVI (1941), 190.

[44] *Canon Law*, 76.

[45] Mary Cheney, "The Compromise of Avranches," *EHR*, Vol. LVI (1941), 190.

[46] *History of English Law*, I, 125 f.

[47] R. R. Darlington, Review of A. L. Poole's *From Domesday Book to Magna Carta, 1087–1216*, *EHR*, Vol. LXVII (1952), 564.

they hardly aspired to elsewhere: namely, an exclusive jurisdiction over testamentary causes and over the distribution of
goods intestate. On the other hand, there were two points at
which the English church had been singularly unsuccessful. The
privilegium fori was confined within unusually narrow bounds,
and secular justice kept a tight hold over all disputes that
touched ecclesiastical patronage.[48]

Ecclesiastical patronage has already been discussed, but a word
should be said about *privilegium fori*. This term refers to
clerical immunity from secular justice, or, as it is more commonly called, "benefit of clergy." Although this principle was
granted in cases of felony, it was, in practice, denied in cases
of personal action. When the king's justices demanded an account of personal or civil actions in the bishop's court, the
bishop, in accordance with canon law, refused to yield the
information and petitioned the pope for confirmation. The
pope acknowledged the request and urged the king to yield,
but he did not confirm the canons. Although clerical privilege
was loudly proclaimed, the state ignored it, and Lyndwood
"could hardly bring himself to give them a gloss."[49]

To return to the theory of decretals that prevailed in the
English courts Christian during the later Middle Ages, were
these decretals accepted as statute law as a matter of course,
or, as was generally assumed by writers of the nineteenth century, did the English church exercise the right to accept some
and reject others? Not only did nineteenth-century historians
hold emphatically to this assertion, but for them it was proved
and no longer debatable. When Maitland began to look for
proof of this assumption, there was none to be found. The

[48] *Canon Law*, 58 f.
[49] *Ibid.*, 61.

topics discussed above are usually understood to serve as proof of this basic assumption. The rule that a bastard cannot be legitimatized by the marriage of his parents evolved in and was enforced by the secular courts. The laws concerning criminous clerics and advowsons were also forced upon the church by secular power, although the church was required to take notice of them and obey them. These instances cannot be accepted as proof of the existence of a national canon law. Maitland contended that as proof of the existence of a national canon law, "we must see an ecclesiastical judge, whose hands are free and who has no 'prohibition' to fear, rejecting a decretal because it infringes the law of the English church, or because that church has not 'received it.' " Further, to be conclusive, this proof must come from the period before the break with Rome, for to rely upon evidence from a later period is to beg the whole question.[50]

Maitland could only conclude that the evidence would not support that statement which said that the treatment which was accorded Roman canon law in the Church of England before the break with Rome was substantially the same as that accorded to the said law after that event. He was not content to rest his case on this negative note, but proceeded to positive arguments in support of his interpretation. After this sudden catastrophe the spiritual courts were expected to enforce, and that without complaint, the "statutes of the temporal legislature, acts of parliament."[51] Secondly, not only must the ecclesiastical courts enforce a new law but they must accept a new

theory about the old law, and it is in substance just that theory the truth of which is here in question. Henceforth a statutory

[50] *Ibid.*, 81, 84, 89.
[51] *Ibid.*, 90.

orthodoxy will compel all judges to say that it was only "by their own consent" that the people of this realm ever paid any regard to decretals or other laws proceeding from any "foreign prince, potentate, or prelate." What is more, these same statutes will eloquently inculcate a free criticism of the old law—nay, a contempt for and a righteous indignation against certain portions of it.[52]

As a result of the great change, some laymen became ecclesiastical judges. This was not as significant as the fact that these new judges would support the new concepts of ecclesiastical law which Henry VIII and his parliaments had propounded. Basic to the decisiveness of the transition was the prohibition of the academic study of canon law. It was intended that the tradition of the fathers should be forgotten. There is "evidence in English libraries, in old catalogues, in medieval wills, and in university statutes" which will prove that young canonists in the Middle Ages were well versed in "foreign literature, in the Decretum and Decretals, in the works of Hostiensis and the archdeacon, of William Durant and Johannes Andreas." It is not likely that men who were so well versed in foreign canon law, in the absence of an English counterpart, would feel free to "criticize, dispute, and deny the first principles of the science that they had so laboriously acquired." In the absence of positive information of this nature, it cannot be assumed that these pre-Reformation canonists considered the three papal law-books as "manuals" rather than as "codes of statutes." It seemed to Maitland, therefore, that there was adequate justification for believing that a new doctrine about decretals was introduced into the spiritual courts of England in the reign of Henry VIII.[53]

[52] *Ibid.*, 91.
[53] *Ibid.*, 92, 98.

THE PAINTED CHAMBER WHICH WAS USED BY EDWARD III
FOR HOLDING A PARLIAMENT IN 1364.

A Medieval Ecclesiastical Court

When Maitland began to work on the subject of canon law in England, Bishop Stubbs, having both lectured on it at Oxford and compiled a memorandum for the Royal Commission on Ecclesiastical Courts, was the only authority in the field. As has been shown in this chapter, Maitland reversed the former opinions on the subjects in such a forthright and conclusive manner that even Bishop Stubbs himself acknowledged the validity of his conclusions.[54] All writers who have approached this general subject in the last fifty years have either begun with or assumed the general conclusions at which Maitland arrived. *Canon Law in England* created excitement and even resentment in Anglican circles, but Maitland's conclusions have held their ground.

[54] William Stubbs, *Seventeen Lectures on the Study of Medieval and Modern History*, 335: "I would refer my readers for this purpose [the criticism and correction of Stubbs's views] to Professor Maitland's recent work on the *Canon Law*. I have so great respect for his knowledge, critical insight, and fairness, that I would gladly submit to any amount of adjustment of facts and authorities that he might prescribe to me."

V

TOWNSHIP
AND BOROUGH

Maitland was in part directed to the subject of township and borough through reading the works of French and German historians who wrote on the origins of towns in their respective areas. His earliest published views appeared in *The History of English Law*[1] and in a review of Keutgen's *Untersuchungen über den Ursprung der deutschen Stadtverfassung.*[2] Maitland's approach here as elsewhere was influenced by the general theme which pervaded all of his writings—the history of English law. His expanded views appeared in both *Domesday Book and Beyond*[3] and the Ford Lectures for 1897, which bear the title of this chapter.

Many questions have been asked of the documents which illuminate this subject. Many, perhaps most, historians have sought from the documents the earliest roots of cities as we know them today. Historians have been too present-minded and not enough historically-minded. They have not sought the truth for its own sake, but have approached the evidence from

[1] I, 634–88.
[2] *EHR*, Vol. XI (1896), 13–19.
[3] Pages 172–219.

a particular tangent or with a hypothesis which they were trying to substantiate. Maitland must bear his share of guilt in this respect. Partial knowledge, while being true in and of itself, may still lead to false impressions. It is at this point, as we shall see, that Maitland's conclusions must be revised.

Maitland began in good juristic style by posing a legal problem. "What is it that makes a borough a borough?" For him this has nothing to do with trade or aggregates of population but is the simple question, Why were some vills separated from others and called boroughs?[4] By the fifteenth century, the answer has become clear and simple to him. "The borough community is corporate; the village community is not." Corporate towns are the result of royal charters. The first definite instance of municipal incorporation is believed to be a charter granted by Henry VI to the men of Hull in 1439.[5] However, Professor Gross has shown that, in essence, incorporation began a century earlier, though not spelled out in specific, legal terms.[6] This can be only a partial answer to the question, for we read of *burhs* in Domesday Book and even in Anglo-Saxon documents.

As well versed as Maitland was in the documents on this subject, it was apparent to him that township and borough were two definite and distinct quantities. Many who have followed him in the investigation of the borough do not seem to have either seen or accepted the distinction which he made. The concept conveyed by the word "borough" was something almost entirely different in the thirteenth and fourteenth centuries from that in the ninth and tenth centuries. A distinction must be made between the Anglo-Saxon borough which

[4] *Domesday Book and Beyond*, 173.
[5] *Township and Borough*, 18.
[6] Charles Gross, *Gild Merchant: A Contribution to British Municipal History*, I, 93 ff.

existed in each shire as a place of refuge, a local market, and a place where business transactions could be duly witnessed and the commercial cities which emerged at important cross-roads, river fords, and harbors in the thirteenth and four-teenth centuries. This distinction is partly obscured by the fact that many of the latter developed upon the sites of the former, although, of course, the situation did not warrant this in other cases.[7]

There is no question but that Maitland was familiar with the results of Continental scholarship upon the origin of towns and boroughs. In spite of this knowledge, however, he rejected most of the conceptual suggestions of Continental historians as they might apply to England. His reasons, so it seems, are two in number. In the first place, Maitland was dealing primarily with the Anglo-Saxon borough, whereas Continental writers seemed to be referring to later developments which accompanied the increase in commercial activity. Further, since he could not find sufficient evidence to substantiate their conclusions, he repudiated them as not being applicable to England.[8]

Maitland tells us that for at least a century and a half before the Norman Conquest, English law had distinguished the borough from the ordinary *tun* or vill. "The typical borough has been (1) the *burh,* (ii) the *port,* and (iii) the moot-stow of a shire."[9] The evidence contributed by the Domesday survey revealed to Maitland that in each county throughout the larger

---

7 "Many of our greatest cities were but rural manors in William I's day, for new discoveries and changing habits have necessitated new centers. But all our modern county towns and many others can look back over a long history to the Saxon past."—D. M. Stenton, *English Society in the Early Middle Ages,* 157.

8 "The Origin of the Borough," *Collected Papers,* III, 31–42.

9 *History of English Law,* I, 636.

part of England there was one, and in general only one, town which deserved special treatment since it was not located on either the *Terra Regis* or land belonging to any man and hence stood outside the land-tenure system.[10]

The Anglo-Saxon documents used the word *burh* to describe what later came to be called a borough. We know that the Germans used this word to describe fortresses which were usually located on hilltops as places of refuge but were unoccupied in times of peace.[11] This concept was undoubtedly carried to England by the German invaders. A *burh* meant only a fortified place and carried with it no hint of a thick population or, for that matter, any population at all. It seems evident that many of these fortifications gave their names to neighboring villages. This fact, however, fails to explain the 250 villages, not to mention hamlets, whose names end in "burgh," "borough," or "bury," in which there is no evidence of either an ancient camp or dense population.[12] The oldest laws reveal that the palisade or entrenchment around a great man's house was a *burh*.[13]

The Danish invasions brought home with force the need for the establishment of strongly fortified towns.[14] "Within a few years burgs were 'wrought' or 'timbered' at Worcester, Chester, Hertford, Witham in Essex, Bridgnorth, Tamworth,

[10] *Domesday Book and Beyond*, 178.

[11] Stephenson, "The Anglo-Saxon Borough," *EHR*, Vol. XLV (1930), 202-203.

[12] "Origin of the Borough," *Collected Papers*, III, 36.

[13] *Domesday Book and Beyond*, 183.

[14] "Borough or fortress towns were garrisoned as a permanent feature of the military scheme, apparently in imitation of Danish usage. In 895 the Danes were defeated by the borough forces (*burhware*) of Chichester. It is clear from the *Anglo-Saxon Chronicle* that in the reign of Alfred's successors new boroughs served as military bases for the conquest and occupation of the Danelaw, and that the Danes held out in similar centers."—William A. Morris, *The Constitutional History of England to 1216*, 77.

Stafford, Warwick, Eddisbury, Warbury, Runcorn, Buckingham, Towcester, Maldon, Huntington."[15] Maitland failed to note the fact, now widely acknowledged, that increasing trade, with the accompanying need for secure markets and places for the storage of merchandise, was also a factor in the establishment of fortified towns.[16] In fact, he specifically repudiated this whole idea as being inapplicable to the "legal essence" of the early borough:

> The mere "market town" is one of the things that we contrast with the borough. For all legal purposes it is a village; it has only the constitution of a village, but once or twice a week a market is held in it. Then, again, the borough as such has no market; the right to have a market is a separate "franchise," which ought to have a charter behind it.[17]

Maitland was so taken up with his search for legal arrangements that he saw only that for which he was looking and regarded anything else as unnecessary. Economic historians have had little concern for, interest in, or understanding of the legal implications of the origin of the borough, while Maitland rejected something which seems so obviously necessary that it does not require elaborate documentation.

The essence of Maitland's theory regarding the origin of the borough can be found in the idea that each shire should have its borough and should take its name from the borough.[18] Lady Stenton has elaborated this concept. As the Danelaw was reconquered, the Danish fortifications at Cambridge, Nottingham, Northampton, Huntingdon, Leicester, and Derby

---

[15] *Domesday Book and Beyond,* 186.
[16] D. M. Stenton, *English Society,* 158.
[17] "Origin of the Borough," *Collected Papers,* III, 35.
[18] *Domesday Book and Beyond,* 187.

were made county-towns or boroughs for the newly laid-out shires. Outside of Wessex the arrangement of borough and shire attained a precision of organization, whereas the existence of royal manors made this impossible in Wessex.[19] The special peace of the king resided not only in the shire boroughs, but in every place that the king either owned or visited occasionally. In noting the presence of a county town in each of the newly constituted shires, Maitland asked, "Have we not here the outcome of a deliberate policy? Is not each district to have its stronghold, its place of refuge?"[20]

Although Maitland denied that the market was a significant cause for the creation of the early boroughs, he readily admitted that once boroughs were established, markets appeared within them. The third function of the borough was to serve as the meeting place of the "moot-stow of the shire," and, perhaps because it was the county's town and was located in no hundred, it had a court of its own which was equal with the hundred-moots.[21] Maitland would hasten to add that all three of these characteristics need not apply to all boroughs, for it would be impossible to make generalizations which would apply in all instances. "Little could be said of Canterbury and Lincoln that would be true of Birmingham or of Brighton." It seemed to him that in 1086 throughout a wide portion of England there were no boroughs which were not in some distinct and legal sense the chief towns of shires.[22]

Maitland explained the distinction between a township and a borough exclusively in terms of defense. We have examined the premises which led him to conclude that the early *burh* was primarily a fortress. Although many would supplement

[19] D. M. Stenton, *English Society*, 158.
[20] "Origin of the Borough," *Collected Papers*, III, 37.
[21] *History of English Law*, I, 636, 637.
[22] *Township and Borough*, 36.

this factor with the impact of the local market and trade, none would deny the importance of the factor which he emphasized. It is at just this point that Maitland loses his followers and supporters. Since a borough among other things is a fortress, obviously it must be garrisoned and kept in repair. Maitland emphasized what he called "the tenurial heterogeneity of the burgesses." Other historians have generally referred to this as "Maitland's garrison theory."

> The fact that we would bring into relief is this, that normally the burgesses of the borough do not hold their burgages immediately of one and the same lord; they are not "peers of a tenure"; the group that they constitute is not a tenurial group. For rather we shall find that, though there will be some burgesses holding immediately of the king, there will be others whose titles can be traced to the king only through the medium of other lords. And the mesne lord will often be a very great man, some prelate or baron with a widespread honor. Within the borough he will, to use the language of Domesday Book, "have" and "hold" a small group of burgesses, and sometimes they will be reckoned as annexed to or as "lying in" some manor distant from the town. It seems generally expected that the barons of the county should have a few burgages apiece in the county town.[23]

What Maitland was trying to tell us was that those who lived in a shire should maintain the borough of the shire because they reaped the benefits which it had to offer. Thus the "haws" or town houses in Winchester were attached to manors in all corners of Hampshire, at Wallop, Clatford, Basingstoke, Eversley, Candover, Strathfield, Minstead, and elsewhere. In terms of Maitland's concept of Domesday Book as principally a geld

[23] *Domesday Book and Beyond,* 178 f.

book, this implies that the town houses were obliged to pay their taxes in the places at which "geld" or tax was assessed. These early boroughs were distinct from townships because they were neither on the king's land nor on land "held" by anyone else. After citing many examples, Maitland concluded that this "tenurial heterogeneity" seemed to be common to all those ancient boroughs which were sometimes called county-towns. In the later Middle Ages, when these towns successfully petitioned the king for "liberties," they were called royal boroughs or the king's demesne boroughs.[24]

Although Maitland's theory is imaginative, it is now generally rejected. The thesis was taken up by Adolphus Ballard, who systematized it and carried it to its logical conclusions,[25] which revealed clearly the weakness of the whole theory. There is no reason to assume that the obligations which fell upon the landowners of the shire for the maintenance of the garrison of the borough "produced the borough's tenurial heterogeneity. The composite character of the Old Roman cities, Canterbury and Rochester, can be traced back at least to the seventh century."[26] Maitland's theory that the inhabitants of each county ought to contribute to the upkeep of the garrison does not explain the references in the Domesday Book to houses "appurtenant" to manors which are not situated in the same county as the borough in which the houses are located.[27] Although both Maitland and Ballard found a particular significance in the fact that borough properties were usually attached to estates in the same shire, Stephenson and Tait suggested that the connection was geographical rather than politi-

---

[24] *Ibid.*, 180, 182.
[25] *The Domesday Boroughs.*
[26] Stephenson, "The Anglo-Saxon Borough," *EHR*, Vol. XLV (1930), 203.
[27] Charles E. Petit-Dutaillis, *Studies and Notes Supplementary to Stubbs' Constitutional History*, 81.

cal, since county lines were disregarded whenever the borough lay close to one of them.[28] Many borough "haws" do not appear to be attached to any manor, perhaps because they were owned by lords who had no other property in the vicinity.[29] If Maitland's thesis be valid,

> Why is it impossible to establish a proportion between the number of burgesses furnished by a manor and the extent of that manor, and how is the fact to be explained that a single manor of the church of Ely maintains eighty burgesses at Dunswich? Why are there so many manors exempt from the burden of maintenance, why are there only three which have duties toward the town of Chester?[30]

These questions simply cannot be answered by his thesis. Ballard's statement that the attachment of borough "haws" to rural estates exactly coincided with, or was necessitated by, the new era of fortification certainly does not throw any helpful light on the subject.[31] The land-books, instead of revealing the systematic practice demanded by the theory of Maitland and Ballard, show a haphazard arrangement which seems quite accidental.[32]

Miss Bateson offered a theory which is simpler than Maitland's and far more satisfactory. She suggested that *burgenses* appurtenant to rural manors were nonresident burgesses, who resided in the country but purchased the freedom of the town in the hope of doing a profitable trade.[33] Petit-Dutaillis sub-

---

[28] Stephenson, "The Anglo-Saxon Borough," *EHR*, Vol. XLV (1930), 183; James Tait, "Review of *Domesday Book and Beyond*," *EHR*, Vol. XII (1897), 775.

[29] Stephenson, "The Anglo-Saxon Borough," *EHR*, Vol. XLV (1930), 183.

[30] Petit-Dutaillis, *Supplement to Stubbs*, 81.

[31] *Domesday Boroughs*, 107.

[32] Stephenson, "The Anglo-Saxon Borough," *EHR*, Vol. XLV (1930), 183.

[33] Mary Bateson, ed., *Borough Customs*.

stantiates this by pointing out that the eighty burgesses of Dunwich, appurtenant to a manor of the Abbey of Ely, had probably bought their title in order to be able to buy herring in the borough market to sell to the monks of the Abbey.[34] It seems a bit surprising that Maitland disregarded his own advice and example on this point. He told us that one could not understand English law without comparing it with its Continental counterpart,[35] and yet in this instance he does not give serious weight to the "tenurial heterogeneity" of French and German towns. When similar examples could be found in both of the areas which are now called France and Germany, there seems to be no reason for attributing an absolutely original growth to the English towns.[36]

There is every reason to accept Maitland's views on the founding of *burhs* or fortified places in the time of Alfred the Great and his successors, but we must reject the purely military distinction which he made between the "borough" and the township. We are told that when documents refer to the market of a borough, reference is made to the *port,* but Maitland suggested that "perhaps from the first there might be a port which was not a *burh.*"[37] He was able to show us no examples, and evidently no one else has been able to discover any. All are agreed on the fact that towns did not merely assume the title of borough but that boroughs emerged as the result of a creative act on the part of the king. Even in the days of the creation of the military *burhs* the economic factor must have played a significant part. Except for perhaps a few strategic points, the king must have chosen a trading place to convert

[34] Petit-Dutaillis, *Supplement to Stubbs,* 81.
[35] "Why the History of English Law Is Not Written," *Collected Papers,* I, 488.
[36] Petit-Dutaillis, *Supplement to Stubbs,* 81.
[37] *Domesday Book and Beyond,* 195.

into a defensive center. The first thing we should note is that the special peace of the king was extended to the boroughs. Maitland tells us that this is doubly significant, for not only are acts which would be illegal elsewhere especially illegal here, but acts which would be legal elsewhere are illegal here.[38] Peace is certainly a prime requisite for successful commercial activity.

Lady Stenton has pointed out that the Saxon kings recognized the economic importance of towns by deliberately decentralizing the coining of money in decreeing that every borough should be a minting place. It is only logical to conclude that there would be no need for so many mints unless there was need for coinage. In a purely agricultural society there is little need for coins. A barter system would probably be adequate, or a royal mint, at most, unless there was an "urban" population dependent upon the local market for its food supply as well as other commodities. The king was the lord of every borough of any size.[39] Maitland indicated that the king had decreed that none should buy or sell outside of the legally established borough market.[40] One purpose of this decree was undoubtedly also the purpose of the system of tithings—to prevent cattle theft. One should make his purchases publicly and before witnesses in order to escape accusation of larceny. Another value of the market for the king was the collection of tolls in which he shared. As was noted earlier, it was customary for borough houses to be attached to neighboring manors. A town house was highly to be desired, for it gave the holder access to the borough market. It was also convenient for the great men of the shire to have a town residence

[38] *Ibid.*, 193, 185.
[39] D. M. Stenton, *English Society*, 159, 167.
[40] *Township and Borough*, 40.

for business or feudal duty, which undoubtedly took them to town several times a year.

Regardless of how scholars may interpret the origin of boroughs, most will grant that the legally established borough or county-town was a royal place. It was created or at least maintained as a place of national importance through the payment of *burh-bot*. It was this, so Maitland felt, that kept the borough from being absorbed in the "system of landownership and manorial jurisdiction."[41] Maitland's idea that the borough, because it was a fortress, became a royal center of administration is substantiated by both English sources and analogy from contemporary Continental institutions.[42] The Anglo-Saxon borough was a vill; it was a hundred by itself.[43] The borough court was not founded on tenurial or feudal principles, and it was the borough court which united the burgesses.[44] Tait accounts for this as "the absence of political and military feudalism in Anglo-Saxon England."[45] The borough becomes "incorporeal" and can be let to farm.[46] Since the borough was an independent or distinct hundred within the shire, the sheriff collected for the king his rents, dues, and the profits of the town court.[47]

Maitland saw a perceptible change begin to transpire in the twelfth century as a new town with a capital "T" began to emerge and the old Anglo-Saxon borough started to fade

[41] "The Origin of the Borough," *Collected Papers*, III, 38 f.

[42] Stephenson, "The Anglo-Saxon Borough," *EHR*, Vol. XLV (1930), 203–204.

[43] Maitland, *Township and Borough*, 41; Petit-Dutaillis, *Supplement to Stubbs*, 84.

[44] Maitland, "The Origin of the Borough," *Collected Papers*, III, 40.

[45] James Tait, *The Medieval English Borough: Studies on its Origin and Constitutional History*, 3.

[46] Maitland, "The Origin of the Borough," *Collected Papers*, III, 40.

[47] D. M. Stenton, *English Society*, p. 171; Maitland, *Domesday Book and Beyond*, 204.

away. Some have failed to see this transformation. The dooms of Edgar tell us that borough courts were to meet three times a year, while the *Leges Henrici* state that borough courts were to meet but twice a year.[48] The privileges and organization of some boroughs began to fall outside a national uniform scheme.[49] Most historians will grant that there is a definite relationship between the special peace of the king and the borough court. In the twelfth century there was a reorganization of the whole criminal system of law in England.

In 1130 the burgesses of Lincoln paid two hundred marks of silver and four of gold to hold their city of the king in chief and thus to avoid dealings with the sheriff. It has been shown even from Domesday Book that the king entered into peculiar arrangements with some boroughs regarding taxation and military service. Municipal liberties and organizations were beginning to be introduced through special bargains, and much diversity was to be the result.[50]

The history of the English borough is closely connected with the monarchy, for the dominant position of the king was responsible for keeping most of the county towns directly under royal control. In the twelfth century, however, both lay and ecclesiastical nobles, following Continental examples, began to found new communities.[51] Occasionally the burgesses of a borough created by a magnate obtained a charter from the

[48] Dooms of Edgar, III, 5, in Stephenson and Marcham, *Sources of English Constitutional History*, 19; *Leges Henrici Primi*, VII, 4, in *English Historical Documents, 1042–1189*, ed. by David C. Douglas and George W. Greenaway, 459.

[49] Morris, *Constitutional History to 1216*, 161.

[50] *Ibid.*, 161 f.

[51] Stephenson, "Taxation and Representation," in *Haskins Anniversary Essays*, 305.

king as well. The borough of Wells was created by the bishop of Bath and Wells in the middle of the twelfth century, and King John also granted it a charter. Lady Stenton suggests that the need for money on the part of Kings Richard and John resulted in many towns' securing by means of new charters freedom to control their own affairs and collect and pay their own dues.[52] The granting of these new and more liberal charters opened a gate that could not be closed, so that by the fourteenth century there was little similarity, except for the name and location, between the towns which then were to be found and those before the Conquest. Much of the confusion which has arisen over the origin and development of the borough could have been prevented by refusing to read the concepts of a complex, urban civilization into the records of a more primitive age. Although all of his conclusions are not tenable, by and large Maitland has set a standard for the method by which to approach and evaluate this early English institution.

Maitland asks, "Why should the borough have a court?" The portmoot was an ancient court of justice which was to enforce the king's special peace in the borough. He rejected the idea that it began with the market because the market was a franchise separate from the borough and therefore had a distinct jurisdiction. The borough court did not grow out of the village court, for "in after times the village or township very often had a court of its own, a manorial court." Although the lord of the town might grant it a charter and hence it was called a borough, this is distinct from the ancient boroughs—the county towns.[53] This court (portmoot) was not able to organize the common life of the town, because it was a court, not a legis-

[52] D. M. Stenton, *English Society*, 185, 173.
[53] Maitland, "Origin of the Borough," *Collected Papers*, III, 34, 35, 33.

lature, and as such was bound by the traditions of its origin.[54] Its only source of income was judicial fines, whose distribution was already prescribed, and hence it had no legal means, or right for that matter, to raise money. The Gild Merchant was able to charge initiation fees and dues and hence had an available treasury. In most towns the burgesses were also members of the Gild Merchant, and the membership came to be considered identical in common thought. We should hasten to point out, however, that Gross has shown conclusively that there is no documentary evidence for the existence of a Gild Merchant either during the Anglo-Saxon period or even in the Domesday Book.[55] This was a feature of the towns which emerged during and after the twelfth century. These same documents indicate that the boroughs possessed no political autonomy.[56] Thus we have examined what have appeared to be two false starts in trying to account for communal action. That there was such action is indicated from the granting of charters to the towns by the king. If neither the Gild Merchant nor the borough court was the instigator, what was? As yet no satisfactory answer has been given to this question.

The primary aim of the merchant guild was to further the ends of its members and to exclude strangers from either competition or membership in the guild. We are told that these guilds "are pious or charitable brotherhoods, clubs whose main business is to brew beer and drink it at the common expense; they are not corporations taking part in the government of the town."[57] The records of the Leicester Gild Merchant are the most complete that we have, and they indicate that the guild effectively controlled the wool trade, which was

[54] D. M. Stenton, *English Society*, 177–78.
[55] Gross, *Gild Merchant*, I, 174–91.
[56] Stephenson, "The Anglo-Saxon Borough," *EHR*, Vol. XLV (1930), 196.
[57] Petit-Dutaillis, *Supplement to Stubbs*, 84.

the dominant trading force in the community. Although the king's consent was theoretically necessary before a guild could be established, apparently many guilds sprang up which did not worry about this technicality. In 1180, Henry II seems to have made a special effort to locate these illicit guilds and fine them.[58] Although Maitland did not enter into any controversy in his brief survey of the merchant guild,[59] he did express his views in his review of Gross's *Gild Merchant*.[60]

Let us now return to the question with which we began this chapter: what is it that makes a borough a borough? The question itself implies that there are places called boroughs that Maitland would exclude from his definition. If men engaged in trade and handicraft settled around a market place and paid money-rents to a lord, they were called burgesses, even though the place was not a county-town. There were very few cases before the Norman Conquest in which a village entirely in the hands of one landlord other than the king became a borough. In these few cases the reason for the change may have been that the king as a special favor imposed his *burhgrith* upon the town, thereby augmenting the revenue of its lord.[61]

Maitland was willing to concede that in Wessex there may have been towns which had secured the name and peace of a royal burg during the time of the struggle with the Danes,

---

[58] Stenton, *English Society*, 178, 181. "As to the part played by the Gild Merchant, Dr. Tait takes a middle position between Gross and Professor Stephenson. Whilst agreeing with the latter as to its significance in reflecting the economic progress of the English towns after 1066, he differs from him in carrying back its origin into the Anglo-Saxon period, and maintains that its importance lay in the organization which made possible common action, and a common spirit, in towns that had not yet attained municipal responsibilities."—Helen M. Cam, review of Tait's *The Medieval English Borough*, *EHR*, Vol. LII (1937), 305.

[59] *History of English Law*, I, 664–68.

[60] "Origin of the Borough," *Collected Papers*, II, 223–31.

[61] *Domesday Book and Beyond*, 214.

even though they lacked the tenurial heterogeneity which is the common mark of a borough. It was noted earlier that the house of the king under very early law would entitle a place to take the title of borough because it had the special peace of the king. The name would persist long after the king actually ceased to stay there and there was no real difference between it and other manors or villages of which the king was the immediate lord.[62]

The climax of Maitland's classification of boroughs prior to the Conquest is the ancient borough, which is the only genuine borough. As noted, these county-towns began as *burhs* or fortresses founded by act or charter of the king as a stronghold for the shire in which they were located. They were royal boroughs, for the burgesses had no superior other than the king, and his was the peace which prevailed within their walls and his were the profits of the court and the market. The king was not necessarily the landlord of all the burgesses. Towns might have markets and even a market court, but only a borough had a royal court equivalent to that of the hundred with representation in the shire-moot.

Maitland's distinction between borough and town was a good beginning in the effort to systematize our knowledge of the Anglo-Saxon borough. He tells us plainly that even as early as the time in which the Domesday Book was being compiled, the attributes of the ancient borough of which we have been speaking had either already disappeared or were in the process of going out of existence.[63] This distinction has been challenged,[64] and the challenge has been refuted.[65] Although much investigation has been done upon this subject

[62] *Ibid.,* 216.
[63] *Ibid.,* 216-17.
[64] Carl Stephenson, *Borough and Town.*
[65] Tait, *Medieval English Borough.*

and refinements have been made,[66] the basic premise remains valid.

Thus three major concepts have been contributed by Maitland to our knowledge of the borough: the origin of the borough, its "tenurial heterogeneity," and the distinction between borough and town. There are many minor points on which he commented in passing; some have been maintained and others have slipped away. Most serious writers on these topics begin with Maitland's position as a point of departure. His view of the origin of the borough as a stronghold for the shire has been modified by noting that the stronghold was usually built at a place of trade or a logical site for a market. The concept of the shire's being divided for the support or garrisoning of the borough is now held by no one. His recognition of the distinctiveness of the Anglo-Saxon or ancient borough is still maintained, although many of his related views on the character of this institution have been refined. Maitland himself has suggested an appropriate conclusion to a study of the borough: "The one strong hint that is given to us by Domesday Book and later documents is that our generalities should be few and that, were this possible, each borough should be separately studied."[67]

[66] Bateson, *Borough Customs.*
[67] *Domesday Book and Beyond*, 197.

VI

ORIGIN OF THE VILLAGE

IT SEEMS ALMOST INEVITABLE that the very nature of Maitland's studies should cause him to be drawn into the vortex of the conflict which arose among historians concerning the nature and the origin of the English village community. It is to be regretted that historians have fallen into the weakness, if not the error, of seeking a single origin of this important institution. Maitland has ranged himself on the side of those "Germanists," who, like Stubbs, find the key to the development of this important English institution in the evolution of Anglo-Saxon society. Seebohm has gone to another extreme in his "Romanist" emphasis on the primacy of the facts prior to the Anglo-Saxon invasions.[1] As the complexity of these early ages becomes more apparent to us, the concept of multiple causation seems more judicious than relying almost entirely on any single factor. The eclectic method of Vinogradoff seems to be the only approach which is capable of leading to a real solution.[2]

Maitland began by telling us that by the time of the Norman

[1] Frederick Seebohm, *The English Village Community.*
[2] Sir Paul Vinogradoff, *The Growth of the Manor.*

Conquest, England was already divided into vills.[3] The division of England into counties, hundreds or wapentakes, and vills revealed the geographical basis of the Domesday survey. While the Domesday Book is arranged in part on a geographical basis, it also contains feudal or proprietary elements, according to Maitland. He adds that while it deals with the counties separately, lands within each county are arranged under the names of the tenants in chief who hold them. When Domesday mentions a place, Maitland assumed it to be a vill, although at the same time it might be a manor. Speaking generally, such a place would later be called a vill and in modern times a civil parish.[4] Maitland concluded that in southern England, the parish normally coincided with the vill, whereas in northern England the parish was larger and included several villages or townships.[5] By the Elizabethan Poor Law the state assumed a function which had previously been carried out by the church and hence adopted the geographical division of the church.

Two problems occurred to Maitland as he studied the geographical arrangement of the vills of Domesday Book. Land is spoken of as a movable thing; it can be moved from one vill or hundred and caused to lie in another. Therefore, one cannot be certain that specific hides or acres really and physically lie in the place in which they are said to lie. This might cause the omission of the names of small vills in certain cases. A second cause of difficulty is the fact that in "comparatively modern times, from the twelfth century onward," two or three contingent villages often have the same name and can be distinguished only by their surnames.[6] Where two modern neigh-

[3] Pollock and Maitland, *The History of English Law*, I, 560.
[4] *Domesday Book and Beyond*, 10, 12.
[5] *History of English Law*, I, 560 f.
[6] *Domesday Book and Beyond*, 10, 13, 14.

boring villages have the same name, Domesday does not treat them as two. It is obvious that many of these names imply a great ecclesiastical organization while others are the family names of families which arose in England either immediately following the Norman Conquest or at an even later date. In some cases it seems almost possible to see the process of fission or subdivision at work. In others it may not be unreasonable to assume that towns always had compound or double names. Maitland concluded that the township or vill of very ancient times was much larger than that of the Middle Ages or the more modern civil parish.[7] The ancient vill, therefore, may have approximately the size of a hundred. Maitland pointed out that there may have existed not only "nucleated villages" composed of one cluster of houses,[8] but also "discrete vills" composed of scattered fragments. Each of these scattered clusters of houses often had a name of its own, and yet only one gave its name to the whole vill. Besides the vills there were hamlets which seemed always to lie within a vill and refer merely to a geographical area rather than to the people who might live within it.[9]

We should not assume a uniformity for English vills. Distinctions are apparent in point of time as well as in geographical position. A description of a thirteenth-century vill should not be applied to the eleventh century. Feudalism will have made certain distinctions necessary. Maitland noted that there are differences between the eastern shires of England and those of the west. The density of population decreases as one moves from east to west. This implies more populous vills and hence a higher value on land in the east than in the west. In

[7] Maitland, "The Surnames of English Villages," *Collected Papers*, II, 91, 90, 93.
[8] *Domesday Book and Beyond*, 15.
[9] *History of English Law*, I, 561–62.

western counties there were at the time of the Domesday survey many vills whose entire land was held by one tenant in chief while the opposite was true in the eastern counties.[10]

The Domesday Book made a distinction between the *manerium* and the *villa* even in cases where the two may have coincided. Maitland has given a detailed account of the Cambridgeshire hundred of Wetherly, which at the time of the Domesday survey contained twelve "true villages."[11] There were sokemen who were not under seignorial justice.

> . . . we should go far astray if we imposed upon these Cambridgeshire villages that neat manorial system which we see at its neatest and strongest in the abbatical cartularies. The villages do not become manors. The manors are small. The manors are intermixed in the open fields. There are often freeholders in the village who are not the tenants of any lord who has a manor there. A villein of one lord will be the freeholder of another. The "manorial system" has been forced upon the villages, but it fits them badly.[12]

Maitland went on to say that the historian must recognize the existence of the free, lordless village as one of the normal phenomena of the time of the Norman Conquest.[13] Some effort must be made to account for this. These free villages existed just as normally as those which were completely subject to a lord. There is every reason to believe that the same basic agricultural practices prevailed contemporaneously in both types of villages. The open-field system, co-aration and the eight-oxen plow team were in common usage.[14] It seems apparent from

[10] *Domesday Book and Beyond*, 20, 22.
[11] *Ibid.*, 129, 131–36.
[12] *Ibid.*, 136
[13] *Ibid.*, 141.
[14] Professor W. O. Ault questions the universality of the eight-oxen plow team.

the Domesday Book that the existence of free villages or towns was not contemplated by the Norman rulers. The Domesday commissioners required the testimony of the priest, the reeve, and six *villani* of every vill. Between the time of Edward the Confessor and the Domesday inquest the sokemen of Orwell had been suppressed to the status of *villani*. The Normans seemed to be consolidating their manors and creating demesne land where none existed before, trying to make every vill a manor. By the thirteenth century the foreigners had done their work so completely that little trace remained of what had been swept away.[15]

Maitland would not allow the free villages much organization in the age of Edward the Confessor. It is doubtful that they had a court and it is questionable whether or not they even had a head-man, reeve, or elder. The area of the village's jurisdiction was probably what later centuries designated as village by-laws: regulation of the arable land, woods, meadow, and waste.[16] We are warned against the temptation to draw inferences about free villages from villages of the thirteenth century which are no longer free.[17] Maitland followed Stubbs in holding that the earliest village communities had no jurisdiction, and any contentious proceedings were carried directly to the hundred court.[18] Maitland further contended that we "underrate the automatism of ancient agriculture and of ancient government."[19] Once the agricultural system went into operation, it did not need to be enforced or reorganized. Each must simply do his share or starve, and this was pressure enough without any more formal arrangement. Maitland in

[15] *Domesday Book and Beyond*, 129, 149.
[16] *Ibid.*
[17] Maitland, *Township and Borough*, 24.
[18] Stubbs, *The Constitutional History of England*, I, sec. 13.
[19] *Township and Borough*, 25.

his reaction to the reading of thirteenth-century organization back into an earlier period seems to have gone to the opposite extreme of oversimplification. Lack of specific reference forces us all to argue from inference on this point,[20] but certainly there must have been some understanding among the householders of these vills regarding agricultural and communal arrangements, regardless of how simple or informal they may have been.

A question basic to the topic of this chapter seeks to determine whether the early history of England began with a population of independent free men or with a population of dependent serfs. Those who hold the latter view[21] would trace the English manor back to the Roman villa and would think of England as being cultivated by men who were either slaves or serfs bound to the soil. Those who hold the former position[22] would postulate the existence of a large number of free men who tilled their own soil and who bore arms in the national host or fyrd. Maitland mentions a variant of this last doctrine which would place the "ownership of the soil or of large tracts of the soil, not in these free peasants taken as individuals, but in free village communities."[23]

The theory that would derive the English manor from the Roman villa must account for the evidence presented by Domesday Book concerning the most populous section of England at the time of the Norman Conquest, the northern and eastern counties. In this area there were many men who were free but were subject with their land to various degrees and modes of seignorial power. In village after village there were no manors at all. One must not say that a Roman villa never

[20] Ault, "Some Early Village By-Laws," *EHR*, Vol. XLV (1930), 208.
[21] Seebohm and Coote, for example.
[22] Kemble, Maurer, Freeman, Stubbs, and Gneist.
[23] *Domesday Book and Beyond*, 221–22.

came into the hands of an Anglo-Saxon chieftain and was maintained by him, but that this was not a common occurrence can be argued from the survivals of the English language and the names of English villages. If the bulk of this English population had remained Celtic after the Anglo-Saxon invasions, the conquerors would most certainly have assimilated some of the Celtic words, and yet we are told that fewer than ten words can be positively traced to Celtic origin.[24] It does not seem likely that the conquering bands of Anglo-Saxons would suddenly settle down as the dependent serfs of their chieftains in spite of the fact that historians today tend to give a much more prominent place to the chieftains of the Anglo-Saxon society than historians of the last century were wont to do.

For Maitland, then, England was composed of a large class of free peasant proprietors who tilled their own soil. Feudalism was the normal process by which the manorial organization became substituted for peasant proprietorship. Maitland would interpret this transition not as a retrogression but as a process of normal and healthy growth. The processes of civilization are often harsh and cruel, but they make possible "the separation of employments, the division of labor, the possibility of national defense, the possibility of art, science, literature and learned leisure; the cathedral, the scriptorium, the library . . . ."[25]

One of the difficulties which arises, according to Maitland, if one tries to picture free village communities upon English soil, lies in the fact that in times of which we have records the vill or township (words used synonymously) had no court, as such. Medieval Latin is a more precise language than our English, and it makes a distinction between the *villa* and the

[24] *Ibid.*, 339, 222, n. 1.
[25] *Ibid.*, p. 223.

villata, between the town and the township, between the geographical area and the body of inhabitants. This distinction may not always have been maintained but it usually was. "If a crime takes place in the *villa* of Trumpington, the *villata* of Trumpington ought to apprehend the criminal, and may get into trouble if it fails to perform this duty." Although the vill itself may not have a court of its own, the vill may have been a manor and the manor would have had a court. Although there was no legal connection between a vill and a manor, they may, in fact, have been coterminous. The frequency of this coincidence seemed to Maitland to increase as he turned to earlier periods. He accounted for it by suggesting that it was possible to create manors after vills had become a governmental district not to be altered except by the central government.[26] Since the hundred was the lowest judicial unit, a village community without a court was hardly worthy of the name. Maitland's whole purpose in this discussion seems to have been to raise a protest against the abuse of arguments from survivals concerning village communities. He contended that in too many cases we are asked to infer without sufficient investigation that some group of facts, which seem out of harmony with their modern surroundings, are and must be ancient and primitive.[27] The evidence from pre-feudal times seemed to show that the vill or township was an agricultural community but not a juridical community, and therefore Maitland doubted whether the township was ever a free village community.[28]

We have seen that Maitland believed that there were villages without a single lord, although the free villagers may

[26] "Surnames of English Villages," *Collected Papers,* II, 84, 86.
[27] "The Survival of Archaic Communities," *Collected Papers,* II, 314.
[28] "Surnames of English Villages," *Collected Papers,* II, 87.

have commended themselves and their lands to different lords. One can believe in the existence of free villages without accepting free village communities as Maitland has defined these terms. Lawyer that he was, Maitland had to consider the theories or doctrines which would warrant an England with free landowning communities. One widely held theory would attribute landownership to communities before it belonged to individuals. Maitland insisted that the only merit which this doctrine possessed was its "vague elasticity." This theory contrasted communities with individuals and yet was afraid to say bluntly the land was owned by corporations before it was owned by men. As a concept of modern law, this doctrine fills a valuable position, but in the history of law it is not likely that land would be attributed to fictitious persons before it was attributed to real men. Historically, Maitland would put his support behind the concept of co-ownership which is based upon individuals rather than upon fictitious persons or corporations. Modern capitalism has forced sharp legal distinctions upon us, but it seems probable that the sharpness of these distinctions decreases as we retreat into the past. Therefore, if we attribute the ownership of land to communities, Maitland pointed out that it should not be attributed to corporations, for we should be aware of the fact that co-ownership cannot be sharply contrasted with ownership by individuals.[29]

In discussing land as belonging to communities before it belonged to individuals, Maitland raised the question of whether we are talking about ownership or governmental power. The sovereign of Great Britain, he told us, does not own all the land in spite of the dogma that all land is held of the king, nor is eminent domain in the United States "ownership nor any mode of ownership." Governmental power per-

[29] *Domesday Book and Beyond*, 341, 342.

mits the imposition of all kinds of governmental restrictions on the use an owner may make of his land. As far back as Maitland could see, "the German village had a solid core of individualism."[30] Although woods and meadows may have been used communally, rights to their use "ran with" the house and arable strips of the individual. As we have seen previously, Maitland held that it was only the economic affairs of the village landowners which made the vill a unit before the central government began to use the township as a unit for law enforcement and the collection of taxes.

The statute books of the fourteenth century seem in some places to assume that every vill would have its lord. There is much evidence cited by Maitland to indicate a common belief that "normally vill and manor are but two names for one thing: the *villa* of public law is the *manerium* of property law." When the vill and manor coincided, the vill gained a governing body, a representative assembly which met periodically. Those who attended the manorial court represented the township which could be seen giving evidence and judgments, making presentments and by-laws. In such cases the lord's court served a dual function as manorial court and townmoot. By the thirteenth century the terms manor and vill were not equivalent, for each was constituted on different principles. Superficially it might be said that the vill was a public unit for police and fiscal purposes, while the manor was a unit of private law constituting a "complex of proprietary rights and mutual obligations which bind lord to tenants and tenants to lord."[31] Manorial rolls reveal cases in which there was more than one vill in a manor and others in which more than one manor was to be found in a vill.

[30] *Ibid.*, 342, 348.
[31] *History of English Law*, II, 606, n. 3, 605 f., 607.

The problem of the regulation of the internal affairs of the non-manorial vill still remains. As has been noted, the vill had no court of its own nor, so far as Maitland could determine, any other non-feudal intermanorial organization. He refused to project one as a necessary expedient for the execution of the minimal demands that were placed upon the village. Rather, he suggested a permanent arrangement made once for all whereby the communal burdens of the township became "real" burdens. ". . . one manor owes an aliquot share of all imposts exacted from the vill, another manor another share. The duty of sending representatives to the courts has been permanently apportioned. To represent Dodford in Buckinghamshire one lord supplies three men, another the fourth man and the reeve."[32]

By the thirteenth century, the township had certain duties which can be clearly discerned. Maitland listed these in his *History of English Law*. It ought to attend the sheriff's tourn, the coroner's inquest, the court held by the justices in eyre, and the hundred and county courts. It was responsible for seeing that all of its members who ought to be in frankpledge were in frankpledge. It must raise the hue and cry in case of cattle theft, must arrest known or suspected criminals, and must be responsible for guarding prisoners committed to it. These duties could generally be included within the scope of either police functions or the collection of revenues. The township must contribute to the fines and amercements levied upon the county and hundred as well as paying those which were assessed directly upon the township itself. Maitland has told us that most of these liabilities can be traced back into the reign of Henry II.[33]

[32] *Ibid.*, 610–11.
[33] *Ibid.*, I, 564–67.

Now that we have seen the principal ideas which Maitland held concerning the origin and the nature of the vill or township, an effort must be made to give perspective to his conclusions. As we saw at the beginning of this chapter, there are two distinct points of view concerning the origin of the vill. These may be described generally as the "Romanist" and the "Germanist" interpretations. These two positions were reconciled in a satisfactory manner by such historians as Savigny, Eichorn, and Palgrave, although it must be recognized that the information available to them was somewhat limited. Toward the latter part of the nineteenth century these interpretations diverged into antagonistic positions. Vinogradoff tells us that not only was there a resurgence of scholarly interest and investigation in the period of the origins of the village but there also developed a keen competition between French and German scholarship (with the British generally taking the side of the Germans), in which the historians took up the position of their national predilection and followed their bias back into ancient times.[34] Perhaps it took a Russian scholar with no emotional ties to either side to observe that the political feelings of the age following the Franco-Prussian War permeated even historical scholarship. At least one scholar who might have been limited by patriotic ties has risen above such prejudices to agree with the general tenor of Vinogradoff's conclusion—Petit-Dutaillis.[35]

In addition to this element of nationalistic bias, there seems to be another factor which has some relevance in determining the general tenor of the opinion held by scholars of the period under consideration. Is it merely coincidence that Kemble,

[34] Sir Paul Vinogradoff, *Villainage in England: Essays in English Medieval History*, 16.
[35] *Supplement to Stubbs*, 10–26.

Maurer, Freeman, Stubbs, Gneist, and Maitland all find that the "Germanist" interpretation comes closest to satisfying the facts? These scholars were concerned primarily with constitutional, legal, or political developments and therefore approached their sources with a certain set of questions which dealt primarily with formal institutional arrangements and the principles which underlay them. On the other hand Seebohm, Coote, and Vinogradoff were concerned more particularly with economic and social organization and developments. They approached essentially the same sources with a different set of questions and found more validity in the "Romanist" interpretation. While Vinogradoff was able to do a relatively satisfactory job of reconciling these divergent positions, he did find some validity in the Romanist position. Although no attempt will be made here to substantiate this hypothesis, it is suggested as a topic worthy of further consideration.

Following the example of Stubbs, the English historian tended generally to be in the camp of the "Germanists." It was apparently in revolt against the preponderance of this interpretation that Seebohm was inspired to write *The English Village Community*. This work proved to be a direct challenge which could not be ignored because of the skill of the author and the freshness of his ideas. Maitland's discussion of the village community which we have examined above was intended as an answer to Seebohm.[36] Although Seebohm's theory, taken as a whole, has generally been rejected, it did cause the "Germanists" to reappraise their position and make some concessions. Although Maitland's work destroyed part and undermined other portions of Seebohm's case, Maitland

[36] "That in some sort I have been endeavoring to answer Mr. Seebohm, I cannot conceal from myself or from others. A hearty admiration of his *English Village Community* is one main source of this book."—*Domesday Book and Beyond, v. f.*

did adopt Seebohm's method of working back from the known to the unknown. In *Domesday Book and Beyond,* Maitland tried to decipher as much as he could about England before the Norman Conquest from the documents of the Domesday inquest. This is a dangerous method when not used skillfully and leads to many questionable conclusions even in the hands of a judicious scholar like Maitland. Although this book is stimulating and imaginative, it is the least satisfactory of all the principal works which Maitland wrote.

Maitland expressed the hope that Vinogradoff would publish a sequel to *Villainage in England* which would settle the issues in dispute on this general question. He lived to see this wish gratified,[37] although we cannot be certain whether or not he accepted the result, for Vinogradoff's conclusions did not completely substantiate his own. Maitland's faith in Vinogradoff was well placed, however, for Vinogradoff's conclusions are generally accepted as the preferred position today.[38]

Vinogradoff refused to begin his history of the land-holding arrangements of England with the Anglo-Saxon invasions or even with the Roman occupation for that matter, but he traced the roots to the time of the pre-Roman Celts. He did not accept Seebohm's one-sided ideas of a complete and unique organization of the Roman villa, although he gives Seebohm credit for indicating the "points of similarity and of contact between the British and the Continental development on the one hand, and English institutions and their Roman antecedents on the other."[39] According to Vinogradoff, the village community and

---

[37] Vinogradoff, *The Growth of the Manor.*

[38] Carl Stephenson, "The Problems of the Common Man in Early Medieval Europe," *AHR,* Vol. LI (1946), 430. Although Stephenson himself does not agree with Vinogradoff, he acknowledges that Vinogradoff's view is accepted by most recent scholars, including Frank M. Stenton.

[39] Vinogradoff, *The Growth of the Manor,* 87.

the open-field system were of ancient origin and were maintained through invasions and catastrophes because they were humble in nature and were readily adapted to the plans of conquerors without causing them any concern or inconvenience. The pattern of great landed estates was set in the Roman period, although the manor, as such, did not become common until the Anglo-Saxon invaders established a military aristocracy which began to exercise economic and political dominance over the remainder of the freemen. Even Maitland acknowledged the change which took place when the powerful Norman feudal barons replaced the Anglo-Saxon aristocracy following the invasion of 1066. With the dominance of the manorial system, the small free landowner was reduced, as we saw in the case of Orwell, to the status of villeins.

Since the time of Stubbs, Seebohm, Maitland, and Vinogradoff, a great deal of talent and energy has been spent on exploring and trying to decipher the Anglo-Saxon period of English history. It would probably be true to say that today more is known about the Anglo-Saxon period than is known of the "succeeding feudal order."[40] It is at least certain that peasant life in the thirteenth and fourteenth centuries is not described today with the "happy assurance that it was a generation ago."[41] Increased research has necessitated the abandoning of the "normal manorial village," or at least it has been confined to a specific habitat. Maitland had suggested that distinctions existed between the villages in different parts of England. This suggestion has been elaborated and substantiated through the study of geology and botany as well as through historical research. What is today some of the best farmland in

[40] Frank M. Stenton, *The First Century of English Feudalism 1066–1166*, 5.
[41] Nellie Neilson, "England," *The Cambridge Economic History of Europe from the Decline of the Roman Empire*, I, 438.

England was not even used in the Roman period. The heavy clay soil of the Midlands was probably heavily timbered when the Anglo-Saxon invasions began. This type of land could not be used until an open-field type of cultivation was adopted, probably in the seventh century.[42]

The origin of the village has been a prime concern of those who have examined the period of the Roman occupation, as well as of those who examined the period following the Anglo-Saxon invasions. Both groups find that their conclusions are in agreement to a great extent. It has been pointed out that even at the height of the Roman occupation of Britain, the majority of the inhabitants were country folk living either in villages or on isolated farms. There is little doubt that the villages were very primitive.[43] The approximate date of the origin and even the nature of the villages must vary in different areas of the country. It would inevitably lead to error to try to impress our modern concepts of the medieval manor on the land-holding arrangements of Roman Britain. Air photography has contributed much in recent years to our knowledge of the size and shape of the fields which were cultivated in earlier eras. Collingwood and Myres have pointed out that the Roman villas and villages do not exist in the same areas. The villa was an isolated farmhouse standing on its own land, which was not in a village. Those villas that have been excavated reflect Roman culture in their architecture and furnishings. The village, on the other hand, was a group of one-room huts clustered aimlessly within a ditch or fence. The village was self-con-

[42] Frank M. Stenton, *Anglo-Saxon England*, 282.

[43] R. G. Collingwood and J. N. L. Myres, *Roman Britain and the English Settlements*, 208; Neilson, "England," *Cambridge Economic History*, I, 438: "Groups of houses built close together in 'nucleated' form, as Maitland calls it, were long ago established places convenient for intercourse, or sometimes slightly off the ancient roadways in order to avoid the invasion of earlier days."

tained in the sense that the agricultural tracts were divided among the villagers and no one else.[44] The fields of the Roman villages were small, seldom more than an acre in size. The Anglo-Saxons, on the other hand, used an open two- or three-field system. Air photography has presented conclusive evidence of these two types of agricultural systems, and the above explanation seems to be the most satisfactory.

It is almost impossible to trace the assessment of land in an English village from the Domesday survey of the eleventh century backwards to the eighth or seventh centuries. Wherever glimpses can be caught, however, it appears that hides were dealt with in units of round numbers such as multiples of five or ten. Although large numbers of isolated farms undoubtedly existed in England in the eighth and ninth centuries, it was the village which formed the basis for social organization.[45] By the time of the Norman Conquest in the eleventh century, a village community, especially in the Midlands, "consisted of a body of men of various degrees of personal freedom, cultivating, by co-operative industry, open-fields which chiefly belonged to a lord."[46]

We must return to Maitland's admonition to exercise extreme caution in the study of the Anglo-Saxon vill because of the constant danger of reading what is understood of the township of the thirteenth and fourteenth centuries into this earlier period.[47] At the time of the Norman Conquest, villages and

[44] *Roman Britain,* 209–13.

[45] F. M. Stenton, *Anglo-Saxon England,* 284, 283.

[46] Richard Howlett, "Village Communities," *Palgrave's Dictionary of Political Economy,* III, 622.

[47] "We see the village of the thirteenth century. We see it in its extents and its court rolls, with a good deal of organization. But it is no longer a free, a lordless village. Far otherwise; most of its inhabitants are the lord's bondmen, his *nativi.* By a mental process we remove the lord and set the villeins free. Too often, so it seems to me, we make these changes and suppose that

farms varied widely from one part of England to another. One cannot generalize from the state of Norfolk to that of Yorkshire, or even from Kent to Sussex, without making serious mistakes.[48] Maitland's distinction between "discrete vills" and "nucleated villages" is adequate for the classification of the two main types of agricultural settlements. As he indicated, in a nucleated village the houses and buildings were grouped around one or two streets, surrounded by its two or three fields, with the uncultivated land lying beyond. The discrete or scattered village, on the other hand, was really not a village at all, but a loose collection of scattered farmsteads or hamlets, each with its own fields. The nucleated village was the one which historians have usually had in mind when discussing the "open-field system" or the "medieval village." This system was prevalent over all the central part of England which is usually called the Midlands, and may be attributed in part to the geography of the area and in part to the family or clan ties of those who settled there after the Anglo-Saxon invasions.

Although Maitland suggested the existence of an alternate arrangement in other parts of Britain, we still know little about it. The scattered settlement was to be found in the Danelaw, Kent, and East Anglia, as well as in western and northern England, which remained largely Celtic. In East Anglia both systems seem to have co-existed, but the functioning of the settlements in this area is still incompletely understood.[49] Maitland's approach to this whole problem is the one still

all else will remain unchanged, that the organization, the bye-laws, the court, will remain though the lord has gone. But does not the village owe much of its compactness to its lord? His hall has become a center for this little world. If we remove that hall, the village will not be disintegrated, but it will be decentralized."—*Township and Borough*, 24.

[48] H. M. Croome and R. J. Hammond, *An Economic History of Britain*, 4.
[49] *Ibid.*, 10.

generally employed; and yet, although a good deal of work has been done, the results remain meager and the conclusions incomplete.

All together, there has been a great change in the techniques used to explore the origin of the village since the days of Maitland. His interest in the subject initially was to refute the conclusions of Seebohm. Although Maitland employed the technique popularized by Seebohm, that of trying to decipher one period from the documents of a later period, he used the method with great care and warned against the weakness of his conclusions. Those who have heeded his warning as well as his conclusions have not been led astray. His strong Germanic bias was undoubtedly a handicap to his work on this subject; nevertheless, we can agree with Maitland that one must consider the villages of different ages separately, as distinct entities. Moreover, a single theory for the origin of the village will not satisfy all that it known of the different geographical sections of England.

VII

THE SOURCES OF
ENGLISH LAW

THE DEVELOPMENT OF a system of common law is a unique feature of medieval England. Those who have examined and studied this body of law have tried to find in it elements which would indicate that it was derived from some other recognizable body of jurisprudence such as German or Roman law. It was inevitable that Maitland should address his attention to this question as well as to several other interrelated problems. At what period of time did the common law system of England become distinguishable and in what manner was it evidenced? The question of the inroads of Roman law must be faced with almost each generation. The civil law of Rome had a direct bearing on the canon law of the church as well as on the teaching in the medieval universities. Maitland faced squarely the issue of the revival of the study of Roman law in Bologna in the twelfth century with its reverberating echoes throughout Europe, as well as the "Reception" of Roman law which enveloped the German states in the sixteenth century and threatened to set aside all other legal systems in Western Europe.

In the history of English law, there is the fiction that legal memory begins with the coronation of Richard I on September 3, 1189. Maitland suggests that this doctrine can be found in certain statutes of Edward I's reign.[1] Legal memory antedates written records, and Maitland would defend the suggested date as an excellent choice. The known plea rolls go back to the year 1194, and the "feet of fines" begin in 1195. With the reign of Richard I, the Chancery began to keep adequate records on the charter, patent, close, and fine rolls. For more than seven centuries, therefore, English law "has had not only an extremely continuous, but a matchlessly well-attested history, and, moreover, has been the subject matter of rational exposition."[2]

England certainly was governed by a body of law long before the time of Richard I. Our information on the Anglo-Saxon laws and customs is so spotty and incomplete that it is desirable if not absolutely necessary to try to work back from the fuller knowledge of the Norman and even later times. This certainly was the method used by Maitland in *Domesday Book and Beyond*. His main concern for Anglo-Saxon law was to shed light upon the later history of the laws of England. English kings had been issuing dooms with the advice of their wise men for five centuries before the Norman Conquest. These dooms do not in any case seem to be an attempt to construct a complete body of law but merely to regulate or amend an accepted body of custom.[3] For the most part they were written in the native tongue, whereas contemporary laws on the Continent appeared in Latin. Maitland believed that the law which prevailed in England before the Norman Conquest was "almost absolutely free from any taint of Roman law" and was in

[1] *History of English Law*, I, 168.

[2] F. W. Maitland, "English Law," *Encyclopaedia Britannica* (1957), VIII, 564.

[3] *History of English Law*, I, 26 f.

the main purely Germanic law.[4] He issued a challenge to those who would claim a Celtic origin for English law. They should either prove that the Anglo-Saxon invaders adopted particular Celtic institutions or else show similar features of Welsh and English law which could not be duplicated in the laws of the Germans.[5]

Although England is on an island, it does not exist and has not existed in a cultural vacuum or in complete isolation from the dominant elements which have influenced the Continent, although the reaction to these elements has often been unique. The basic Teutonic law of England has been affected by various impacts of Roman law. There have even been arguments among those who contend that some particular Germanic strain—purely Anglo-Saxon, Scandinavian, or Frankish—has exerted the dominant influence upon English law. Maitland rejected the suggestion that Roman law survived the Teutonic invasions by pointing out that even Christianity had to be reintroduced into England in the sixth century. This introduction of the Roman ecclesiastical tradition, which culminated in a system of canon law, was the first important Roman invasion of Britain's "Germanic polity."[6] Probably the English kings were merely following Roman example in collecting their customary laws in writing.

As far as the history of English law is concerned, Maitland would contend that the Norman Conquest took place in 1166 rather than in 1066, because in that year the "decree went forth which gave to every man dispossessed of his freehold a remedy to be sought in a royal court, a French-speaking court."[7] This was significant for two reasons. In the first place,

[4] "The Materials for English Legal History," *Collected Papers*, II, 20.
[5] *History of English Law*, I, xxix.
[6] *Ibid.*, xxxii.
[7] *Ibid.*, 84.

it meant that the king's courts were to be the fount of justice, with resulting centralization, uniformity, and efficiency. It would be more difficult to bribe or to intimidate justices backed by the king, and true justice would have a better chance of prevailing. In the second place, a language which was not the native tongue was introduced as the official legal language. If this language had been Latin, there would have been a strong tendency to turn to the civil law of Rome for rules and precedents. A technical language developed which was adequate because of its ability to express a legal point or concept so exactly that "when slowly French gave way before English even as the language of law reports and legal textbooks, the English to which it yielded was an English in which every cardinal word was of French origin."[8]

William the Conqueror apparently intended to govern England by English law, not even trying to introduce Norman law in its stead. It was an attempt to determine what the laws of England actually were that resulted in such compilations as the *Leges Edwardi Confessoris*. Maitland even suggested that the Normans had no written law at the time of the Conquest of England and little that might be called jurisprudence. What, then, were the Norman contributions to the development of English law? As suggested above, for a long time after 1066 there appeared to be no significant changes in the sphere of law. The most important result of the Conquest for the law of England was the "establishment of an exceedingly strong kingship which proved its strength by outliving three disputed successions and crushing a rebellious baronage.[9] The development of a technical language of the law and the introduction into England of such men as Lanfranc, who was trained in Ro-

8 *Ibid.*, 85.
9 *Ibid.*, 77, 94.

man law, were other significant by-products of the Conquest. A study of English law in the period between the Conquest and the reign of Edward I must certainly take into account the development of canon law as well as medieval Roman law. Lanfranc, whom William I appointed Archbishop of Canterbury and upon whom he leaned heavily, had been trained in the Pavian law school, where Roman law as well as Lombard law was being studied. Before coming to England, Lanfranc had founded the Abbey of Bec, where, at a later time, Anselm received his training. It was during Anselm's tenure of the office of Archbishop of Canterbury that the investiture controversy involving conflict between canon law and English common law arose. Although this influence was indirect and Maitland would hardly consider it, the fact that William had the assistance of a skilled lawyer, trained in the law, undoubtedly contributed to the speedy mastering of the rules of Anglo-Saxon law, which is not unimportant. Another fact which is at least interesting is that the handwriting of the Domesday Book is in an Italian style.[10]

Most scholars agree that although Britain was under Roman domination for a long period of time, "practically nothing is traceable of its effects on our [English] pre-Norman law.[11] Maitland would suggest that there was hardly any visible influence of Roman law upon English law until the middle of the twelfth century.[12] From Bec, Anselm was followed by Archbishop Theobold, who brought Vacarius to England. Vacarius is usually given credit for introducing the academic study of both civil and canon law into England. Stubbs suggested that before the introduction of the study of Roman law into Eng-

---

[10] T. F. T. Plucknett, *A Concise History of the Common Law*, 212.
[11] Percy H. Winfield, *The Chief Sources of English Legal History*, 54.
[12] *History of English Law*, I, 117.

land, "a stream of young archdeacons, at the age at which in England a boy is articled to an attorney, poured forth to the Italian law schools."[13]

It should be noted that the ages of Glanvill and Bracton, or the twelfth and thirteenth centuries, are important in the formulation of the English common law. The mere fact that these men are given credit for writing books on the law, and that these books became standard authorities and were reproduced many times, is in itself justification for considering the sources and nature of their ideas. Beyond this, however, they witnessed the greatest reception of Roman law in English history. The influence of the legal renaissance of the twelfth century was exercised upon the judicial machinery of the state and upon the technical expression of legal rules rather than upon the substance of the rules themselves. Maitland tells us that "Glanvill's work was influenced, Bracton's work profoundly influenced by Roman law."[14] Plucknett suggests that Glanvill's treatise may have been an imitation of "some of the little books of canonical procedure which became frequent at this time."[15] Glanvill apparently anticipated that his readers would have some knowledge of Roman law, for he frequently warned against being misled by superficial resemblances between English and Roman law. This can be illustrated by the use of the Latin word *dos* by the king's court, which he cautioned does not mean the "dowry" of Roman law.[16] Vinogradoff suggested that the real benefit which Glan-

[13] *Seventeen Lectures on the Study of Medieval and Modern History*, 349.

[14] "The Materials for English Legal History," *Collected Papers*, II, 32.

[15] *Concise History of the Common Law*, 212; Maitland makes a similar statement in *History of English Law*, I, 165.

[16] Plucknett, *Concise History of the Common Law*, 212; Holdsworth, *A History of English Law*, I, 203.

vill and Bracton derived from Roman law "consisted in a fertility of ideas about law."[17]

In 1895, Maitland traced the sources of the influence of Roman law upon English law in the thirteenth century, in a volume entitled *Bracton and Azo*. He was inspired in part by his disagreement with Sir Henry Maine, who had said that Bracton "put off on his countrymen as a compendium of pure English law a treatise of which the entire form and a third of the contents were directly borrowed from the Corpus Juris." Maitland did not agree with this statement, and he wanted conclusive evidence with which to refute it. He concluded that the amount that Bracton borrowed directly from the Corpus Juris was not even a thirtieth part of his book.[18] On the other hand, Bracton did borrow from Azo perhaps as much as a fifteenth of the treatise. Early in the thirteenth century Azo stood at the head of the famous school of law at Bologna and was recognized as an outstanding authority on Roman law. Maitland compared the most Romanesque parts of Bracton's treatise with the texts from which they were derived. Although Romanesque in form, Bracton's treatise was found by Maitland to be genuine English law based upon the rules and forms of the royal courts, including references to cases decided there. While generally accepting Maitland's conclusions upon the Roman element in Bracton's writings, Holdsworth suggested:

> The diversity of opinion upon this subject may be perhaps accounted for by the following considerations: we have seen that Bracton's Treatise was written just at the close of the period during which English law had been developed by men who

[17] *Roman Law in Medieval Europe*, 104.
[18] Maitland quoted this statement by Maine in *Bracton and Azo*, xiv.

knew something of the canon and civil law, and just at the beginning of the period when English law was to be controlled by men who knew little except the system which they had passed their lives in applying at the bar or on the bench.[19]

Maitland considered Bracton to be the "crown and flower of English medieval jurisprudence." In 1245, Henry of Bratton was already a justice in eyre and was holding a dispensation granted by William Raleigh and confirmed by Pope Innocent IV for the tenure of three benefices. For a period of about ten years following 1248, he was among the justices who held pleas *coram ipso rege,* and he frequently appeared as a witness to the royal charters along with the great folk of the realm. It was during this period before 1258 that Bracton did the main part of his writing. Maitland has edited a notebook which apparently belonged to Bracton which contains some two thousand cases copied from the rolls of those two famous jurists, Martin Pateshull and William Raleigh. Bracton cited some five hundred decisions in his treatise, and when Maitland compared many of these decisions with the record, he found that Bracton had accurately stated the practice of the king's court.[20]

After his careful scrutiny of Bracton's notebook and his comparison of Bracton's treatise with the writings of Azo, Maitland concluded that although Bracton was "an able man who can write well and fluently about things that he understands . . . he is a poor, an uninstructed Romanist." He went on to point out that in several cases Bracton was apparently trying to paraphrase a point made by Azo, but instead of pointed argument, Bracton "gives us pointless truism or some-

19 *History of English Law*, II, 268.
20 *Ibid.*, I, 206, 209.

thing that is dangerously near nonsense." Bracton cited English cases when dealing with matters which came before the English courts, but looked to Roman sources when dealing with speculative or academic questions to fill what he considered to be gaps in the English law. Bracton was most Roman when he was "studying his note book, weaving a doctrine out of the plea rolls, or dealing with the judgments of Pateshull and Raleigh."[21] There are important voices to be heard, however, which do not agree with Maitland's estimate of Bracton's Romanism. The disagreement seems to hinge on one's estimate of the purpose Bracton had in mind when he drew on rules of Roman law. G. E. Woodbine holds that if Bracton's sole aim was to reproduce the rules of Roman law in their technical sense, then the result is open to criticism; but if he was merely employing Roman material in order to write a complete and systematic treatise on English law, then use of the foreign element was both "intelligent and skillful."[22] Sir Paul Vinogradoff agrees with Woodbine's conclusion.[23] Looking at Bracton's book in the light of subsequent years results in a tendency to overestimate the characteristics of the law which have endured and to underestimate those which did not become permanent. Holdsworth has very ably and judiciously summarized this apparent controversy:

> If the judges who succeeded Bracton had possessed Bracton's knowledge of Roman law, more attention would have been paid and justly paid, to the Roman parts of Bracton's Treatise, because they would have had more influence upon the history

[21] *Bracton and Azo,* xviii, xix, xxi–xxix, xxiii.

[22] "The Roman Element in Bracton's *De Adquirendo rerum dominio,*" *Yale Law Journal,* Vol. XXXI, (1925), 827–47.

[23] "The Roman Element in Bracton's Treatise," *Yale Law Journal,* Vol. XXXII (1926), 751–56.

of English law. The great historical interest of the Treatise is this—that it comes at the parting of the ways. It gives us a picture of English law as developed by judges who were not merely common lawyers.[24]

Maitland tells us that during the thirteenth and early fourteenth centuries the textbooks and manuscripts which were written show that English lawyers were steeped in Bracton. Bracton thus summarized and preserved the common law and emphasized the decreasing effect of the Roman law in England. His influence declined in the fourteenth and fifteenth centuries. Holdsworth believes that the work of Bracton exercised its greatest influence upon modern English law in the sixteenth and seventeenth centuries, when the lawyers of England fortified themselves from Bracton's treatise to fend off the threatening reception of Roman law.[25]

Maitland also gave considerable thought to the subject of the sixteenth-century revival of Roman law. He summarized and developed his earlier ideas upon this subject in the Rede Lecture for 1901—"English law and the Renaissance." Here it was suggested that the death of Rede[26] was a good date for beginning the "second new birth of Roman law." At this time humanism was revitalizing the old Roman law. It is generally conceded that it was at this time also that Roman law was gaining the ascendency over German law in Germany, or at least "forcing it to conceal itself in humble forms and obscure corners."[27]

Maitland's main view was that England was saved from a reception of Roman law in the sixteenth century primarily

[24] *A History of English Law*, II, 244.
[25] *Ibid.*, II, 288 f.
[26] January, 1519.
[27] "English Law and the Renaissance," *Historical Essays*, 137.

as a result of its long-established common law courts and by the system of legal education which had been carried on by the Inns of Court.[28] He firmly believed that the threat to subvert the English common law was both real and serious. In support of this position he cited the beliefs and position of Reginald Pole, the cousin of Henry VIII who became a cardinal, but might have become king of England. Pole recommended that a "wise prince" banish the "barbaric" common law and replace it with the civil law of the Romans. Soon after this, Henry VIII prohibited the academic study of the canon law and founded a professorship in the civil law at Oxford and Cambridge.[29] Maitland further pointed out that Thomas Smith, the man appointed to fill this chair at Cambridge, was a doctor of the Roman law who had received his training at the University of Padua. It does not necessarily follow from the above that either King Henry or Smith, for that matter, desired a reception of Roman law, but Maitland suggests that it does afford a challenge and hence danger to the common law.

Maitland says that "it would not I think be difficult to show that the pathway for a reception was prepared." It was in the year 1535 that the stream of law reports known as the Year Books came to an end. Maitland suggested that during the middle years of the sixteenth century the common law courts had little to do. After the middle of the century, however, there was a revival of English law: "The medieval books poured from the press, new books were written, the decisions of the courts were more diligently reported, the lawyers were boasting of the independence and extreme antiquity of their system." Nothing, in the eyes of Maitland, other than the Inns

[28] "Records of the Honourable Society of Lincoln's Inn," *Collected Papers,* III, 79.
[29] "English Law and the Renaissance," *Historical Essays,* 141, 137 f.

of Court and the Year Books which were read there, could have saved the English common law from a reception of the civil law of Rome.[30]

I cannot find that these ideas represent the best of Maitland's scholarship. The sixteenth century was not the area of his widest knowledge and soundest judgment. It is probable that his attention was drawn to this subject by two events. First, he had been asked to write an article on "The Anglican Settlement and the Scottish Reformation" for the *Cambridge Modern History,* and as he casually gathered material for this article, his attention was called to the fact that Scotland had had a reception of Roman law and England had not. Secondly, he kept informed on current affairs and was very much interested in the reform and codification of the German Civil Code which was going on in his own day. Indeed, he advocated a comparable reform for England.[31] From his interest in these two areas, he tried to find a hypothesis to explain why Germany and Scotland had had a reception and England had not. It was not too difficult to find evidence to support the conclusion, cited above, which presented itself to him. His serious study at this time was with the Year Books, and they seemed to offer the solution to the question at hand. Maitland did not study the sixteenth century carefully and objectively to determine whether the threat was real or only apparent. He was, however, a scholar whose ideas were not to be taken lightly; hence the views expressed in this rather popular lecture were carefully scrutinized by scholars investigating the sixteenth century, and his remarks provided a stimulus to further study of the question that his own answers did not adequately explain.

In a review of Maitland's lecture, Goudy suggested that the

---

30 *Ibid.,* 142, 146, 145.
31 "The Making of the German Civil Code," *Collected Papers,* III, 474–88.

"considerable infusion of Roman law into the English system" which took place at least as early as the thirteenth century was as important as either the Inns of Court or the Year Books in preventing a general reception in the sixteenth century.[32] Professor Holdsworth, who has gleaned the whole field of the history of English law, has attacked Maitland's question systematically. The sixteenth century was indeed a transitional period for England as well as Continental nations. New institutions and courts were created in England[33] or older ones were newly organized which acted upon principles which did not harmonize with the common law. Holdsworth thus agrees with Maitland that a rival system of administration and law presented itself.[34] Holdsworth lists four reasons that have been offered for suggesting that the first half of the sixteenth century was a critical time for the common law:

> In the first place, there is some evidence that the business of the common law courts was declining. In the second place, we hear complaints of the defects in the law, substantive and adjective, administered by the common law courts. In the third place, the Year Books cease to appear. In the fourth place the activity of the new courts and councils is increasing.[35]

He proceeds to examine each of these factors carefully before coming to the conclusion that none of them are conclusive. He points out further that the common law gave Henry VIII most of the powers that he needed and Parliament could confer upon him any that he lacked.[36] Even Henry VIII

[32] EHR, Vol. XVII (1902), 359.
[33] Privy Council, Star Chamber, the Court of Requests, the Court of High Commission, the Council of the North, the Council of the West.
[34] A History of English Law, IV, 218 f.
[35] Ibid., 253.
[36] Ibid., 283.

admitted that England had a constitutional monarchy. The law could be changed by Parliament alone, and yet Parliament owed its strength to the common law, which reinforced its authority. For these reasons, Holdsworth rejected Maitland's contention that the common law was in danger in the first half of the sixteenth century.

Professors Cam[37] and Plucknett[38] accept Holdsworth's views on the question of the reception as being more adequate than the interpretation propounded by Maitland. A revolutionary reception of the Roman law was practically impossible in England. The whole legal system would have to have been swept away or seriously modified, and there were too many persons with vested interests in the existing system for this to happen. That the system was inadequate and needed to be modified brought pressure for reform to meet the needs of the new age. Lawyers turned to the pages of Bracton seeking help for the expansion of the common law. In Bracton's book, which was first printed in 1569, lawyers "came into contact with Bracton's Romanism which they found already adapted, more or less, to common law needs."[39] Thus the reception was nationalistic in character, for the lawyers and judges turned back to the law books[40] of the thirteenth century, which the renaissance of Roman law had inspired, rather than directly to Roman sources. New courts and councils appeared in the sixteenth century which administered civil or canon law, but most of them accepted the general principles of the common law.[41] As the legal system evolved, the new became fused with the old, and no serious attempt was made to replace the old with the new.

[37] In Maitland, *Historical Essays*, 141, n.
[38] *A Concise History of the Common Law*, 214–15.
[39] *Ibid.*
[40] Bracton, Glanvill, Britton, and Fleta.
[41] Holdsworth, *A History of English Law*, IV, 286.

Here, as elsewhere, we have seen that Maitland was not content to ask merely what happened, but went further to try to determine why and how it happened. The question of origin again looms large in this subject. When one ventures into the realm of analysis and interpretation and departs from the security of merely collecting facts, he leaves himself open for difference of opinion or revision based upon more complete information. In discussing the sources of English law, Maitland asked questions and offered answers. He did not even pretend to speak the last word on the subject, but merely hoped to suggest an area and avenue of study which might stimulate others to a more systematic and complete investigation and analysis than he had time or knowledge to render. Thus, while Maitland's conclusions can no longer be accepted as the last word, one should certainly consult him when looking for the first word.

VIII

THE YEAR BOOKS
OF EDWARD II

BROKEN IN HEALTH and sensing that his days were numbered, Maitland turned, even though often from his bed, to a study of the Year Books. Although he was forced to flee England each year for his health, he was able to take photostats of Year Books or even on occasion the actual documents themselves to his winter retreat in the Canary Islands. He had the strength of will and keenness of mind to keep thinking even when his body would no longer respond to his will. Undoubtedly this contributed to his attempt to analyze the grammar of the medieval French in which the Year Books were written. His conclusions were embodied in fifty-five octavo pages in the introduction to volume one of the *Year Books of Edward II* which he edited for the Selden Society.

Maitland was not the first to appreciate the value of the Year Books, nor was he the last. In his concern for the history of English law, he realized that the Year Books must be edited critically before the history of the law could be written for the period covered by them. The task of editing was a dreary and laborious one that required skill as well as industry, though it lacked glamour or promise of material reward. It was difficult enough even to find sufficient money to publish the volumes without thinking of paying the editors. Maitland was willing to forego any remuneration for his work on *The Mirror of Justices,* while another member of the Selden Society defrayed all expenses for publishing *Bracton and Azo* in order that work on the Year Books might progress. Even these generous efforts would have been in vain if it had not been for the annual contributions of the Inns of Court.[1]

The Year Books cover the period from the reign of Edward I until the reign of Henry VIII. As early as 1285 someone was writing down in French the oral arguments which he heard in court. From 1293 until the reign of Richard III, the Year Books flowed in an almost continuous procession. In the reigns of Henry VII and Henry VIII, they became less regular until they ended with the Year Book of the Trinity term of the twenty-seventh year of Henry VIII. The Year Books first began to be printed in the fifteenth century and appeared more or less regularly until 1638. In 1679 there appeared the standard edition of the Year Books, which, although it was purported to be corrected and emended, for the most part simply was a reprint of the Year Books which had been collected and published in the sixteenth and seventeenth centuries. Maitland has exposed the carelessness of the editor of this work.[2]

From 1679 until Horwood began editing the unpublished rolls of Edward I, in 1863 for the Rolls Series, nothing was done about the Year Books. In 1885, L. O. Pike took up where Horwood left off on the rolls of Edward III. He suggested comparing the Year Books with the plea rolls of the common bench and indicated the difficulty which this effort would entail, for

---

[1] B. F. Lock, preface to Vol. IV of *Year Books of Edward II,* ed by the late F. W. Maitland and G. J. Turner, x.
[2] Maitland, *Year Books of Edward II,* I, xxi–xxviii.

there was no index or published calendar for the rolls.[3] "The Year Books are, in fact, to those who know how to use them, the most perfect guides to almost all that is important in the rolls."[4] Maitland acknowledged his indebtedness to Pike for suggesting the proper method of editing the Year Books.[5] In the light of this fact, let us examine Pike's approach to the task in order to see how much Maitland followed Pike and in what particulars Maitland was original.

Pike indicated clearly that the reports which appeared in the Year Books did not come from or represent any single authorized report. In some instances there were several different reports of the same session of the court. There is no indication that one is more official than another. The majority of the cases which are recorded in the Year Books were heard in the court of common pleas. The records which correspond with the reports in the Year Books are to be found on the "Pleas of Judgment Rolls of the Common Bench."[6] These reports were recognized by Pike as being of value for social, historical, and constitutional as well as legal matters. Whereas the rolls or official records contain only the bare essentials of fact, the Year Books are full of "living men dealing with the facts in their own language, in the spirit of their own age, in tones which reveal what manner of men they were."[7] Maitland certainly recognized the importance as well as the truth of the following statement by Pike concerning the Year Books: ". . . owing probably to the difficulties which they presented to

---

[3] "The Manuscripts of the 'Year Books' and the Corresponding Records," *The Green Bag*, Vol. XII (1900), 539.

[4] Luke Owen Pike (trans. and ed.), *Year Books of Edward III*, III, xvi f.

[5] *Year Books of Edward II*, I, *xxi*.

[6] Pike, "Year Books," *The Green Bag*, Vol. XII (1900), 533, 538.

[7] Luke Owen Pike, "An Action at Law in the Reign of Edward III: The Report and the Record," *Harvard Law Review*, Vol. VII (1894), 277.

the unlearned, nothing has been done except incidentally to make their contents, or even the general nature of them known to the public."[8]

Recognizing this fact, Pike set out to do something about the situation. Maitland was later to enter into the labors of his able and worthy predecessor. The Year Books are incomplete in certain important particulars if one would gain the maximum benefit from the information which they do afford. The names of the judges and counsel are indistinguishable or omitted altogether, and the names of the principals are not to be trusted. This information can sometimes be supplied from the plea rolls, rolls or letters patent, or the "feet of fines." Pike wrote an article to illustrate how this material should be used,[9] and Maitland was familiar with this article. Even before Maitland turned to the task of editing the Year Books of Edward II, he indicated that "an edition of the Year Books similar to that which we now have in the Rolls Series for a few lucky years of Edward III [edited by Pike] would be an inestimable gain, not merely to the historian of law but to the historian of the English People."[10]

Although we recognize that Maitland was not the first to produce critical editions of the Year Books, the task was arduous none the less. In addition to producing a critical text and its translation, the thoughtful editor must endeavor to answer certain questions which arise from the very nature of the documents under consideration. Attention has already been called to the fact that Maitland took the occasion "to settle the grammar and syntax of the Anglo-French language, its nouns and its verbs, its declensions and its tenses."[11] Scholars in medieval

[8] "Year Books," *The Green Bag*, Vol. XII (1900), 538.
[9] "An Action at Law," *Harvard Law Review*, Vol. VII (1894), 266–79.
[10] "The Materials for English Legal History," *Collected Papers*, II, 54.
[11] Fisher, *Maitland*, 166.

French have acclaimed this work, and the editors of the *Cambridge History of English Literature* have seen fit to reprint it.[12] Other questions to which other scholars had given answers had to be re-examined so that he might accept or reject their conclusions on the basis of his own investigation. It was necessary to give at least tentative answers to such questions as the authorship, the source, and the purpose of the Year Books.

"Legal writers, from Coke to Blackstone, seem to have believed that the Year Books were compiled by salaried, official reporters," remarked one researcher.[13] Although this view had been abandoned before Maitland turned to the Year Books, his views concerning the authority of the Year Books seem to be the most complete and the most satisfactory exposition on this subject. The widely held belief that the Year Books were official reports seems to rest upon some words of Edmund Plowden, "that great lawyer [who] has told us that he began to study law in the thirtieth year of Henry VIII."[14] Plowden wrote:

> As I have been credibly informed, there were anciently four reporters of cases in our law who were chosen and appointed for that purpose, and had a yearly stipend from the king for their trouble therein; which persons used to confer together at the making and collecting of a report, and their report being made and settled by so many, and by men of such approved learning, carried great credit with it.[15]

At best this is only an indication of hearsay evidence. Mait-

---

[12] A. W. Ward and A. R. Waller, eds. (15 vols., New York, Macmillan, 1939). "The Anglo-French Law Language," I, chap. XX, 455–60.
[13] Charles C. Soule, "Year Book Bibliography," *Harvard Law Review*, Vol. XIV (1901), 557–87.
[14] *Year Books of Edward II*, I, xi.
[15] Quoted by Holdsworth in *A History of English Law*, II, 532.

land detailed several difficulties in the way of the acceptance of the Year Books as official reports. If reporters had been appointed by the king, one would expect to find their appointment recorded and some mention of their salary on the fiscal roll. Such records are to be found for royal judges. Further, Maitland suggests that if the reports had been official, the original copy would have been preserved; yet our only manuscripts have come from private hands.[16] If an official document had been copied, an attempt would have been made to make an exact copy; yet where two or more copies do exist, they are very unlike. From this circumstance Maitland drew the conclusion that the Year Books were the notebooks of apprentices or learners. Before examining his conclusion, however, we should take a second look at Plowden's statement quoted above. Holdsworth agrees with Maitland that Plowden's statement rested "merely upon report; and the statements of later authorities are merely amplifications of his words."[17] Sir Frederick Pollock has suggested that Plowden's words probably do not even refer to the Year Books, but are merely a "rhetorical excuse for his shyness in publishing his own reports."[18] Pike has suggested that a modified form of the old tradition may be true.[19]

His theory is based on the conjecture that Plowden's tale of the four men appointed and paid by the king to draw up reports, and Blackstone's tale that these reports were drawn up by the prothonotaries, though incorrect as they stand, are founded upon a combination of two sets of correct facts. He thinks that the four clerks, whom he identifies with the *Custos Brevium* and

[16] *Year Books of Edward II*, I, xii.
[17] *A History of English Law*, II, 532.
[18] *Ibid.*
[19] *Year Books of Edward III*, 20 (Rolls Series), II, lxix–lxxx.

the three prothonotaries of later days, may have been employed by the king to enter official records in the court of Common Pleas, and that each of these clerks made the separate unofficial reports which have come down to us in the Year Books. These two sets of facts, he thinks, were combined by Plowden and Blackstone; and thus there emerged the tale that the Year Books were composed by four official reporters paid by the king.[20]

Holdsworth has rejected Pike's theory because "it fails to explain the characteristics of the whole series of Year Books."[21] Pike's theory has also been rejected by two more recent editors of the Year Books—Bolland and Turner.[22]

"It is difficult to discover in the Year Books anything which throws light on their history."[23] By means of internal criticism, Maitland arrived at the conclusion that the Year Books were compiled either by or for those who were interested in learning the law: "Only thus can we account for some of those facts which will be given in evidence hereafter." Apprentices had a great deal to learn and few means of learning it. The best, if not the only, way to learn the law and the legal processes was to attend the sessions of court and listen to what was said. The educational process would be speeded by taking notes, borrowing and copying notes, and discussing each other's notes. Accepting the Year Books as student notebooks would explain the apparent freedom to omit, curtail, condense, or even to expand the reports.[24] The official record was

[20] Holdsworth, *A History of English Law*, II, 533 f.
[21] *Ibid.*
[22] F. W. Maitland, L. W. V. Harcourt, and W. C. Bolland, eds., *The Eyre of Kent*, xxv–xxviii; Maitland and Turner, *Year Books of Edward II*, IV, xxv–xxviii.
[23] Soule, "Year Book Bibliography," *Harvard Law Review*, Vol. IV (1901), 568.
[24] *Year Books of Edward II, III*, xii, xiii.

concerned with keeping an exact record of the proceedings in each case and contained no arguments or pleadings but those which the court accepted. The reports, on the other hand, contained the reasons and arguments for those pleadings which were rejected as well as for those which the court allowed.[25]

The Year Books, as has been suggested, contained reports rather than records. Maitland tells us:

> When all has been said that it is fair to say of England's wealth of legal records, the truth remains that the history of English law from the days of Edward I to the days of Edward VII must be primarily sought, not in records properly so called, but in reports. To this may be added that in the way of intellectual products medieval England had nothing more purely English to show than its law reports, its Year Books.[26]

These law reports were for the use of members of the legal profession, even including the judges.[27] It was not unusual for practicing lawyers to sit in on a case which had special legal significance. The law reports show the general principles of law, pleading, and practice. Cases were not recorded for their intrinsic value but only as they illustrated or contributed to matters of general interest. This would explain the haphazard use of names and places. Just as the lawyer studied books of precedents of writs and pleadings in order to present his case in proper form, so he studied the Year Books to see what principles the court had applied in the past.[28] The Year Books were rarely, if ever, actually cited by counsel or judges. It would not have been logical to cite unofficial sources which might

[25] Pike, "An Action at Law," *Harvard Law Review*, Vol. VII (1894), 266.
[26] *Year Books of Edward II*, I, ix.
[27] Pike, "An Action at Law," *Harvard Law Review*, Vol. VII (1894), 266.
[28] Holdsworth, *A History of English Law*, II, 537 f.

vary or even conflict; nevertheless, the court would tend in most cases to follow its own precedent unless there was just cause for a change. Maitland illustrated this by reference to the report of a case in 1454 in which Prisot, C. J., pointed out that a certain point had been decided a dozen times "in our books," and if these precedents were disregarded, young apprentices "who are studying in 'terms' . . . would never give credence to their books."[29] This certainly implies that case law is the result of rather than the cause of the law reports. The Year Books, written by lawyers, for lawyers, are the most importance source of and authority for medieval common law. There is an inherent weakness in this source, however, for the reporter would not record anything which was common knowledge, but primarily the principles which were either new or were being reinterpreted. Therefore, we moderns find it difficult to think the unexpressed thoughts of the medieval lawyer which are no longer a part of legal tradition. Even Maitland, in honesty, had to admit that "we do not hope to make good sense of all the reports that we publish and shall not always feel ashamed when we fail."[30]

The Year Books were written in neither Latin nor English but in French. Maitland reported that the quality of the French, in general, was poor. This he interprets as an indication of its genuineness. It may indicate that the reporter wrote down the conversation as he heard it without attempting to embellish or correct it. "We fancy that learned men who explore the history of the French of Paris would sacrifice many a *chanson de geste* for a few reports of conversation that were as true to nature, as true to sound, as are our Year Books." The language in which the Year Books were written resulted in

29 Maitland, *Year Books of Edward II*, III, *ix, xv.*
30 *Ibid., xciii.*

the development of a legal language, for the French words could more aptly convey the exact sense of meaning demanded by the very nature of law itself. Maitland went so far as to say that the English common law had to "borrow a word corresponding to almost every legal concept that had as yet been fashioned." The technicality of the language of English law was a source of its strength. It is his conviction that if the language of English law had been more English and less technical, it would have been swept aside in the sixteenth century by the general reception of Roman law. The language of English law did undergo a transformation between the time of Edward II and that of Henry VIII: "A single case of Henry VIII's day shows us 'deer, hound, otters, foxes, fowl, tame, thrush, keeper, hunting.' We see that already the reporter was short of French words which would denote common objects of the country and gentlemanly sport."[31] In the Middle Ages French was the language of society even when English was the native tongue. A person would be more likely to write French than English.

In various places, Maitland has expressed his views on the general value of the Year Books. One of his succinct expressions is widely quoted: "Our 'formulary system' as it stood and worked in the fourteenth century might be known so thoroughly that a modern lawyer who had studied it might give sound advice, even upon points of practice, to a hypothetical client." Here he has indicated that a complete picture of the working of the law is presented or preserved in the Year Books. Not only is the legal system itself revealed with its many facets, but light is shed on the "thoughts and sayings and doings of a class of men who played a part in English history which is by no means insignificant."[32]

---

[31] *Ibid.*, I, *xvii, xxxv, xxxvi, xxxvii.*   [32] *Ibid., xvii;* III, *xciv.*

As we have seen so many times, Maitland's vision far out-reached his grasp. Not content to work along as a journeyman contributing his own relatively small portion to the immense task, he called for a national edition of the Year Books:

> What we want is a new and a worthy edition of the Year Books undertaken as a national enterprise. We want a dozen men trained or in training to do the work: trained, if need be, at Paris under masters of the old French language; trained, if need be, at Harvard under masters of the old English law. It will cost money. It may fill a hundred perhaps two hundred volumes. But we must have it, or England, Selden's England, will stand disgraced among the nations.[33]

This was a dream, but Maitland was more than a mere dreamer. Governments are generally run by politicians and not by scholars. The outlay of money involved in Maitland's proposal would not have won much support even if his plan had been incorporated in a bill and introduced into Parliament. Maitland caught a vision of the possibility of carrying out his project at a more leisurely pace through a privately sponsored organization. It was through the inspiration of Maitland and the support of some of his friends, who had become infected with his enthusiasm, that the Selden Society was formed in 1887 "to encourage the study and advance the knowledge of the history of English law."[34] One of the many projects of this organization has been to sponsor the editing and publication of the Year Books. Maitland set the pattern in his editing of four volumes of the *Year Books of Edward II* for the Society.

[33] *Ibid.*, I, *xxxii* f.
[34] Plucknett, "Frederick William Maitland," reprinted from the *NYU Law Review*, Vol. XVI (1951), in *Maitland Reader*, 195.

At the beginning of this chapter there was mentioned the personal sacrifice which Maitland was willing to make in order to get the initial volume of the *Year Books of Edward II* published. In reality, the cost to him was actually much greater physically than financially. When the obstacles were finally surmounted and the first volume appeared in 1903, Maitland's "brilliant introduction to that volume captivated the legal and historical authorities of England, America, France, and Germany, and assured the popularity of the series."[35] Maitland's efforts on behalf of the Year Books were not in vain, for the Selden Society continues to fulfill the dream which Maitland could not hope to complete himself.

Although many volumes of the Year Books have appeared since the death of Maitland, the editors have builded on the foundation laid by Pike and Maitland. None have addressed themselves to the questions which Maitland asked and answered. Recent editors have edited and analyzed the reports in terms of their content and intrinsic value, but have apparently seen no need to review Maitland's conclusions concerning the origin of the Year Books and the uses to which they can be put by modern scholars.

[35] Lock, preface to *Year Books of Edward II*, IV, xi.

IX

THE ELIZABETHAN
RELIGIOUS SETTLEMENT

MAITLAND, AS WE HAVE SEEN earlier,[1] had been drawn into conflict with Anglican protagonists over the question of Roman canon law and the early English church. Once again he found himself involved in a religious problem, fraught with emotional overtones—the Elizabethan religious settlement.

We noted previously Maitland's apparent aloofness from partisan religious feelings, but whatever his "personal predilections were, his passion for historical truth and his legal exactness made him a papalist when determining an issue long obscured by ecclesiastical controversy."[2] In *Roman Canon Law in the Church of England,* Maitland had presented a convincing case for his position that Roman canon law had been accepted as authoritative in English ecclesiastical courts until the time of Henry VIII, unless specifically controverted by royal authority. The impartiality with which he handled this emotionally fraught subject was undoubtedly the reason for his being invited by Lord Acton to write a chapter for the *Cambridge Modern History* on the Elizabethan settlement.[3]

[1] Chapter IV, above.
[2] Cam, in *Historical Essays,* xx.

146

This chapter with its by-product, "Elizabethan Gleanings," caused Maitland to be drawn further into conflict with the defenders of the high Anglican position regarding the English Reformation.

The problem at hand can be confined arbitrarily to Elizabeth's accession to the throne and the activity of her first Parliament in 1559. Before examining the interpretive contributions of Maitland and their ramifications, however, we should set forth the chronology of the events to be interpreted.

Queen Mary's end did not come as either a shock or a surprise. "The bells which six years before had rung in triumph for Mary's accession, now pealed as merrily for her death."[4] The only group who may not have been happy over the prospects of a new queen were the Roman Catholic extremists. Each group optimistically saw in the new, young queen the fulfillment of their desires and wishes. Even those who could not be enthusiastic had to concede that at least this was better than another "War of the Roses." None knew exactly what to

[3] "The Anglican Settlement and the Scottish Reformation," in II, 550–99. "That Acton should have chosen Maitland for this particular piece of work may cause some surprise. The ground was intricate, sown with pitfalls and clouded with controversy, and Maitland had made no special study of the sixteenth century upon the political side. On the other hand he could bring to the task a cool, dispassionate judgment, a fine power for appraising historical evidence, and a singular and exact felicity in the expression of delicate shades of certainty and doubt. That he stood outside the churches might have been a disqualification, had devotional impulses been the staple consideration in the question, or if the banners of rival confessions were not already waving on the battle field; but the age of Elizabeth was theological rather than religious, and it was of the first importance to obtain the verdict of a thoroughly impartial mind upon a subject which could never be treated by a churchman without some suspicion of partisanship attached to his results. Maitland accepted the task with misgivings, and discharged it with characteristic thoroughness."—Fisher, *Maitland*, 104 f.

[4] James Anthony Froude, *History of England From the Fall of Wolsey to the Death of Elizabeth*, VII, 2.

expect from the new queen, and all religious factions made a play for her favor.

Elizabeth was plunged into the midst of a formidable situation. There had been three religious upheavals in England in a generation, and the English people were bitterly divided over religion. Elizabeth's position was further complicated by a European entanglement which found England associated with Spain in the Hapsburg-Valois rivalry. French troops occupied Scotland, where Mary of Guise ruled as regent for Mary Stuart in the interests of France. Mary Stuart claimed the English throne, and there was always the possibility that French troops might be used to make good her claim. So long as Philip II of Spain clung to the hope of marrying his sister-in-law, he would not permit any French coup in England. The situation was further complicated by the empty royal treasury and the disintegration of the armed forces. Elizabeth had a statutory title to the throne based upon her father's will and an unrepealed statute in her favor.[5] This was more than enough to counterbalance the challenge to her legitimacy.[6] "The only alternative to Elizabeth was the Queen of Scots; her accession would mean virtually the conversion of England into an appanage of France."[7] English nationalism was too strong to permit this to occur.

Elizabeth was admirably prepared both by temperament and by experience for such a situation. Not in vain had she lived for the past six years in the shadow of the Tower; a hasty

[5] Maitland, "The Anglican Settlement," *Cambridge Modern History*, II, reprinted in *Historical Essays*, 163.

[6] "If the succession to the throne had gone by mere heredity, then strictly speaking Mary was the nearest heir, for not only was Elizabeth illegitimate by Catholic Canon Law, but, until Parliament could meet, she was also illegitimate by English Law."—J. E. Neale, *Queen Elizabeth I*, 64.

[7] Arthur D. Innes, *England Under the Tudors*, 244.

action or thoughtless word might have spelled her doom. She had learned to depend upon her own judgment, to hide her true feelings, to act with moderation, and to speak with indirection. Lytton Strachey suggests that this was her salvation.

Such was her nature—to float, when it was calm, in a sea of indecisions, and, when the wind rose, to tack hectically from side to side. Had it been otherwise—had she possessed, according to the approved pattern of the strong man of action, the capacity for taking a line and sticking to it—she would have been lost. She would have become inextricably entangled in the forces that surrounded her, and, almost inevitably, swiftly destroyed.[8]

This was undoubtedly the impression that she desired to create. One is nevertheless left to wonder if she was not "dumb like a fox." Her experiences as a child growing up amidst swift political change and sudden reverses of fortune "converted her plastic and unformed mind into the calculating machine it afterwards became."[9] When messengers bearing letters hailing her as the "miraculously preserved champion of the truth" arrived, she greeted them with the noncommittal text: "This is the Lord's doing and it is marvellous in our eyes."[10]

Even before her coronation, Elizabeth faced the question of religion. The choice of William Cecil as her secretary was an indication that England would be Protestant. The first important proclamation forbade any attempt to alter the established order of religion. The obvious purpose of this measure was to calm the anxieties of her Roman Catholic subjects by

[8] *Elizabeth and Essex*, 13.
[9] J. B. Black, *The Reign of Elizabeth, 1558–1603*, 2.
[10] Maitland, "The Anglican Settlement," *Historical Essays*, 168.

quieting the rabid Protestant preachers, but some astute observers came to the conclusion that the measure was intended to silence the subjects but reserve to the crown the right to introduce its own innovations.[11] In effect, this postponed any decision upon the state religion until Parliament should meet. It was also noted that instead of the title "Supreme Head" at the close of the queen's style, there stood an innocent-looking "etc.," and later, when the same abbreviation appeared on the writs of summons to Parliament, it became clear that she had given up the disputed title "Supreme Head."[12]

Maitland has written what is probably the best examination of Elizabeth's title and its importance. For him, Elizabeth was the first English sovereign to bear the title "etc.," which was to be used for nearly two and one-half centuries. As has been pointed out, this "etc." appeared in Elizabeth's first public document at the end of the Queen's titles, where in her father's and brother's reigns the title "Supreme Head of the Church" had been. Maitland asked, "Had this phrase always been meaningless? I venture to suggest that it had its origin in a happy thought, a stroke of genius."[13] J. B. Black agrees that "it was no ordinary brain that devised so clever a subterfuge."[14]

Elizabeth was confronted by a difficult problem. The statutes of Henry VIII had declared that the headship of the church was annexed to the throne by divine law as well as by act of Parliament. One of Queen Mary's statutes had gone to the other extreme by declaring, in effect, that her father's eccle-

[11] Black, *The Reign of Elizabeth*, 7.
[12] W. H. Frere, *The English Church in the Reigns of Elizabeth and James I, 1558–1625*, 2 f.
[13] "Elizabethan Gleanings: Defender of the Faith, and So Forth," *EHR*, Vol. XVIII (1930), reprinted in *Collected Papers*, III, 157–65.
[14] *The Reign of Elizabeth*, 8.

siastical supremacy had been null and void all along. Elizabeth had subjects who held tenaciously to both opinions. At this juncture she hit upon the brilliant idea of "etceterating herself."[15]

It was both a bold and a cautious step; bold, because implicitly it maintained the theory of the English Reformation that the supremacy of the Papacy was a usurpation of the crown's ancient authority, and that no parliamentary statute was needed to confer the headship of the church on the monarch; cautious, because, after all, no more appeared than the words "et cetera," which left the Catholic world guessing and hoping about the future.[16]

The uniqueness of Elizabeth's title, according to Maitland, was the fact that she added "et cetera" to an otherwise unabbreviated style which contained all the other titles borne by her father and brother. Maitland traced the use of this form to a scribbled memorandum, preserved in the Record Office and dated November 18, 1558, the second day of Elizabeth's reign.[17]

Maitland's view has not gone unchallenged. Hubert Hall was the first to differ with Maitland's explanation of "et cetera."[18] and two years later A. F. Pollard pointed out that Mary had used "etc." until March 26, 1554, when her triumph over Wyatt made it possible for her to dispense with her supremacy over the church.[19] Even though Elizabeth was not

[15] Maitland, "Elizabethan Gleanings," *Collected Papers*, III, 159.

[16] Neale, *Queen Elizabeth I*, 63.

[17] "Elizabethan Gleanings," *Collected Papers*, III, 161, 164.

[18] *The Athenaeum*, May 2, 1908, p. 543.

[19] A. F. Pollard, *The History of England from the Accession of Edward VI to the Death of Elizabeth, 1547–1603*, 192.

the first to use the "etc.," Maitland's explanation of why she used it needs no modification.

Elizabeth's personal religion is a subject central to this whole discussion. Most writers seem to agree that "of religious feeling, in the ordinary sense of the word, she probably had little."[20] Strachey would even go so far as to imply that Elizabeth was Protestant only by accident of birth, for basically she was so secular that she became the champion of the Renaissance rather than of the Reformation.[21] Maitland dissents from the tenor of these remarks, holding that "at the critical time her conduct was swayed rather by her religious beliefs than by any close calculation of loss or gain."[22] Being a dissenter from all religions himself, Maitland has apparently been generous in giving Elizabeth the benefit of the doubt—too generous. J. B. Black's conclusion seems more valid:

> Her cold, entirely humanist outlook, nourished by classical study, kept her apart from the deeper spiritual currents of her time. Moreover, she had seen too much of the ravages of fanaticism, both Protestant and Catholic, to set any store by the dogmatic formularies of either side. The only religious faith she can be said to have held with any degree of conviction was a belief in an over-ruling Providence—the refuge of all distressed human beings.[23]

Elizabeth's theological views were inclined toward Luther and the Augsburg Confession rather than toward Calvin. "For herself she would have been contented to accept the formulas which had been left by her father, with an English ritual, and

[20] Black, *The Reign of Elizabeth*, 3.
[21] *Elizabeth and Essex*, 14.
[22] "The Anglican Settlement," *Historical Essays*, 167.
[23] Black, *The Reign of Elizabeth*, 3.

the communion service of the first Prayer-Book of Edward the Sixth."[24]

Strong nationalist that she was, Elizabeth, feeling confident that her subjects, both Roman Catholic and Protestant, leaned toward an independent church, accepted the break with Rome as a fundamental condition of her religious establishment.[25] At one time it was believed, even by von Ranke, that Elizabeth had left the Roman Catholic church as a result of her harsh treatment at the hands of Pope Paul IV.[26] Although this interpretation had been quietly dropped by historians, it had not been openly refuted until Maitland undertook the task. Such a story was believed because it seemed plausible, for "the Pope, Paul IV was an irascible old man, from whom the last quality to be expected was moderation."[27] A real danger existed that the Pope would declare Elizabeth a bastard, England a papal fief, and her assumption of the crown an insolent usurpation. As a result of such treatment, Elizabeth was supposed to have decided to break relations with the papacy and follow the desires of her Protestant subjects. Maitland set the record straight. After carefully outlining Elizabeth's actual dealings with Rome, he concluded:

> Whether Paul ever made any attack against Elizabeth on the score of her birth is very doubtful. That he never made any public and solemn attack against her on that score, or even on the score of heresy and schism, is fairly certain: many would have preserved copies of a bull that denounced her, whether as heretic or as usurper. But at least it should be indubitable that

[24] Froude, *History of England*, VII, 12.

[25] Conyers Read, *The Tudors: Personalities and Practical Politics in Sixteenth Century England*, 149 f.

[26] Maitland, "Elizabethan Gleanings," *Collected Papers*, III, 165.

[27] Neale, *Queen Elizabeth I*, 64.

she was not driven into Protestantism by his insults. Apparently he did and said nothing against her until he learnt that she was withdrawing her minister from his court, and that her talk of sending an embassy had been deceitful.[28]

Elizabeth's first Parliament met in January, 1559. Although the influence of the crown was used on the side of Protestantism, no circular letters were issued such as Mary Tudor had employed in vain in her efforts to keep Protestants out of her House of Commons.[29] This was not a packed legislature,[30] although the "Queen took the ordinary precautions permissible in her day for facilitating the passage of government measures."[31] Some would even go so far as to imply that this body may be taken to represent a fair cross-section of national sentiment.[32] Maitland suggests that, by and large, the nation was willing to follow Elizabeth in the experimental religious settlement.[33]

Parliament opened on January 25, and for the first time Elizabeth stood as queen face to face with her subjects. Sir Nicholas Bacon, Keeper of the Great Seal, gave the speech from the throne. When the business session began on Monday, the thirtieth, the question of supply came first before the legislators. Money was cheerfully voted, and Parliament turned next to a discussion of a royal marriage. In response to the suggestion that she choose a husband, Elizabeth replied that she preferred to remain unmarried. Two statutes were passed

[28] "Elizabethan Gleanings," *Collected Papers*, III, 166, 173 f.
[29] John E. Neale, *Elizabeth I and Her Parliaments, 1559–1581*, 38.
[30] C. G. Bayne thoroughly demolished the old legend that Elizabeth's first parliament was packed. "The First House of Commons of Queen Elizabeth," *EHR*, Vol. XXIII (1908), 455–76, 643–82.
[31] Black, *The Reign of Elizabeth*, 10.
[32] Read, *The Tudors*, 15.
[33] "The Anglican Settlement," *Historical Essays*, 172.

to answer the question of Elizabeth's legitimacy. Parliament now turned to the topic of ecclesiastical supremacy, which everyone recognized as the chief task of this session. Three bills were introduced in the succeeding months before a settlement could be reached.

On February 9, the "Bill to restore the Supremacy of the Church of England to the Crown of England" was introduced in the Commons and had its first reading. J. E. Neale has attempted to determine what happened both in and out of Parliament to Easter, 1559, which might explain the final form of the Acts of Supremacy and Uniformity.[34] After this date the passage can be followed satisfactorily by means of Maitland's "diplomatic."[35] Since Neale failed to discover any new evidence, his task was that of analyst rather than of researcher.

Neale contends that very significant factors entered the English political scene between the introduction of the first government bill and the third one which eventually became the law of the land. He hypothesized that Elizabeth intended to follow the example of her father and brother in introducing changes in the English church gradually or by stages rather than all at one time. This procedure was suggested by prudence as well as by the international situation. He would have us believe that the Queen's program encountered well-organized and deliberate opposition in the House of Commons from the Marian exiles or their supporters.[36] After the Commons had rejected the first government supremacy bill, it introduced a substitute of its own based on the Edwardian set-

[34] "The Elizabethan Acts of Supremacy and Uniformity," *EHR*, Vol. LXV (1950), 304.
[35] "Elizabethan Gleanings," *Collected Papers*, III, 185–209.
[36] Neale, "The Elizabethan Acts of Supremacy and Uniformity," *EHR*, Vol. LXV (1950), 312–22. "The Commons had risen as a body in a gesture of open defiance" (p. 322).

tlement, which was amended by the Lords. Rather than sign this supremacy bill, Elizabeth issued a proclamation based upon it, which authorized communion in both kinds, on the Wednesday of Holy Week.[37] Neale suggests that after this, either Thursday night or Friday morning, Elizabeth had a sudden change of mind, which he attributes to her receipt of the news of the Peace of Cateau Cambresis.[38] Elizabeth now felt that her position had been consolidated to the place where she could grant to the Commons what they wanted immediately and what she had hoped to secure at some future date— an act of uniformity and a prayer book. This novel interpretation, while admittedly based upon conjecture, does not do violence to any known facts and certainly warrants consideration along with the traditional account.

Before Parliament reconvened after the Easter recess, a colloquy was held at Westminster which featured a disputation between champions of the Roman Catholics and of the Protestants. Maitland suggested that the outcome of the debate raises suspicion that it was merely a trap laid by the Protestants for the purpose of discrediting the Roman Catholic faith.[39] As a result of the disputation, the bishops of Lincoln and Winchester were committed to the Tower, and thus the Roman Catholic party in the House of Lords was seriously weakened at a critical moment.

Parliament went back to work. The basic outline of the Elizabethan settlement appears to have been drawn, and only the details were left to be determined. Elizabeth decided that she would not assume the title of head of the church, but would accept a substitute phrase which declared her to be "the only

[37] Frere, *The English Church*, 18, 22.
[38] Neale, "The Elizabethan Acts of Supremacy and Uniformity," *EHR*, Vol. LXV (1950), 324.
[39] Maitland, "The Anglican Settlement," *Historical Essays*, 173.

Supreme Governor of the realm as well in all spiritual or ecclesiastical things or causes as in temporal, and that no foreign prince or prelate had any ecclesiastical or spiritual authority within her dominions."[40] The Act of Supremacy was finally passed on April 29. On the preceding day, an Act for the Uniformity of Religion had been enacted.

Let us now examine the effect of these new measures. The Act of Supremacy revived the anti-papal statutes of Henry VIII, removed Mary's reactionary legislation, and vested the supreme power over the national church in the crown. The oath of supremacy was compulsory for all clergy, judges, mayors, and royal officials under pain of debarment from offices in church and state. If any person "shall by writing, printing, teaching, preaching, express words, deeds, or act . . . defend the authority . . . of any foreign prince, prelate, person, state, or potentate" within her majesty's dominions, he should suffer on the third offense death for high treason.[41] The Act of Uniformity imposed a slightly modified version of the second Edwardian Prayer Book. The ritual of the communion service was modified by the addition of two sentences which seemed to admit the Real Presence in the sacrament.[42] This may have been done either to conciliate the Lutheran princes of Germany or to appease the English Roman Catholics. Clerical offenders against the Prayer Book were subject to life imprisonment for the third offense, while the laity were to be fined 12 d. for each absence from church.[43]

Moderation is certainly the tenor of Elizabeth's religious

[40] *Ibid.*, 175.
[41] Stephenson and Marcham, *Sources of English Constitutional History*, 345, 346.
[42] Read, *The Tudors*, 150.
[43] Stephenson and Marcham, *Sources of English Constitutional History*, 347 f.

settlement. The obvious effect that could be seen was the use of English in place of Latin in the church service. Actually there was a demand from Roman Catholics as well as Protestants for the Bible in the vernacular. J. B. Black tells us that Queen Mary had a difficult time in getting Roman Catholics who had come into possession of English Bibles during Edward's reign to give them up.[44]

Pope Pius IV prohibited "good" Catholics from participating in the worship of the English church. Maitland has examined the efforts of the Roman Catholics in England to persuade the Pope to reverse his decision on this matter. Froude brought transcripts of the documents involved back to England from Simancas in Spain. The Spanish ambassador in England, Alvaro de Quadra, wrote to the Spanish ambassador at Rome, Francesco de Vargas, on August 7, 1562, asking for an authoritative decision regarding the legality of attending the English services and setting forth reasons for granting the desired permission.[45] The false claim was made that the penalty for failure to attend "common prayers" was capital punishment, when actually it was only the fine of 12 d. Every effort seems to have been made to persuade the Holy Father to give the desired answer. The Pope replied without equivocation that if the choice lay between attending the forbidden services or going to the gallows, death would be the better portion.[46]

[44] *The Reign of Elizabeth,* 19.
[45] "Elizabethan Gleanings," *Collected Papers,* III, 177–80.
[46] "Ad casum respondemus quod neque vitam catholicam relinquere, nec hereticam ducere, neque eorum psalmis, lectionibus et concionibus interesse licet: cum in casu proposito non esset cum hereticis communicare et cum eis participare sed vitam et errores illorum protestari, cum non velint aliam ob causam interesse nisi ut tanquam heretici reputati poenas catholicis impositas effugiant; et scriptum est obedire oportet Deo dicenti Qui me erubuerit et meos sermones, quanquam hominibus vitam et ritus Deo et ecclesiae con-

The settlement was instituted with little or no open opposition and almost no persecution. It succeeded in securing the support of the great majority of the English people, although extremists on both sides were undoubtedly dissatisfied with the arrangement. "It is a tribute to the enduring qualities of the settlement that in looking back it has seemed natural and inevitable: as though from the beginning there could have been no other policy than that of the middle-way—the *via media* of tradition."[47]

While investigating the Elizabethan religious settlement, Maitland decided to examine the original documents of the Acts of Supremacy and Uniformity to see if he could learn "something from the external aspect of the parchment and the work that had been done thereon by pens and knives."[48] After going over the same material, J. E. Neale vouched that Maitland had done the task so thoroughly that he left "scarcely an 'i' to be dotted."[49]

Maitland was able to determine the chamber in which each of the sections of the final bill of the Act of Supremacy originated as well as certain changes or amendments which were made in the process of enactment.

On the whole, then, as fairly certain conclusions, we may hold (1) that the Commons sent up a measure consisting of sections I–XVII, XXII, and XXIV: (2) that the Lords add sections XX (restriction of the scope of heresy), section XXI (requirement of two witnesses), and section XXII (aiding and comforting offenders), and at the same time cancel certain parts of

trarios praecipientibus, et eo magis cum nobiles et magnates non sine pusillorum scandalo supradictis interesse possint."—*Ibid.*, 179.

[47] Neale, *Elizabeth I and Her Parliaments*, 51.

[48] "Elizabethan Gleanings," *Collected Papers*, III, 185.

[49] "The Elizabethan Acts of Supremacy and Uniformity," *EHR*, Vol. LVX (1950), 304.

sections XV and XVIII, which the new clauses have made unnecessary; and (3) that the commons at the last moment add section XIX, declaring that no act in this present parliament shall be adjudged to be "any error, heresy, schism, or schismatic opinion."[50]

Maitland next suggested a solution to the mystery of why Elizabeth did not sign the second bill of supremacy which was passed by both chambers during Holy Week. He thought that it either declared Elizabeth to be the supreme head of the church or else gave her the embarrassing option of declaring whether or not she was the supreme head. When the bill, "having passed both houses, was no longer amendable, she decided (or for the first time published her decision) that she would not assume the irritating title." Viewing Elizabeth's decision not to sign this bill into law against the international scene, Maitland found another evidence of the Queen's astuteness. On April 24, Philip II of Spain informed his ambassador in England that since Elizabeth had refused the supreme headship when it was offered to her, he had told the Pope that there was still hope for her amendment, and he tried to prevent the issuance of a decree concerning her legitimacy.[51]

The Act of Uniformity disclosed less than the preceding parchment. Maitland noted that the enabling clause did not contain the usual "lords spiritual and temporal" phrase which had appeared even on the Act of Supremacy which had abolished papal jurisdiction and repealed the Marian statutes. He believed that the omission was probably an accident.[52]

It has long been known that the Journal of the House of Lords contains no record for the days on which the third

[50] "Elizabethan Gleanings," *Historical Essays*, 238.
[51] *Ibid.*, 238, 239, 240.
[52] *Ibid.*, 244.

supremacy bill and the uniformity bill were passed by that house—April 22–May 1. Maitland made a fruitless examination of the original journal in the hope of throwing light on the omission. The question which came immediately to his mind, of course, was whether the omission was the result of accident or fraud. It might be suggested that not one lord spiritual voted in favor of these bills and that the Queen's ministers did not want this to be a matter of record. Such speculations are worthless, however, since they can neither be proved nor disproved.

According to Maitland, Pope Pius IV not only had no serious thoughts of "denouncing Elizabeth as an excommunicate heretic and deposed queen, [but] made at least four attempts to secure her conversion."[53] Three of these efforts are well known, but Maitland endeavored to make a case for the fourth attempt. In chronological order, the efforts of Vincent Parpaglia in 1560, Martinengo in 1561, and the Cardinal of Ferrara in 1562 have been widely reported. Thomas Sackville was in Rome in the winter of 1563–64, where he was arrested as a spy but was soon liberated. A letter from Cecil indicates that Sackville may have been secretly commissioned by Elizabeth. A later letter from the Spanish ambassador in England to King Philip relates an account of the conversation of the Pope with Sackville.[54] According to this account, the Pope wanted to assure Elizabeth that if she would make dutiful submission, she need not fear being deposed as illegitimate or prevented from marrying whomever she pleased.

Maitland found two additional Roman transcripts at the Record Office which bear on this tale. The first was a certificate of respectability in Sackville's favor, dated at the English hos-

53 *Ibid.*, 180 f.
54 *Ibid.*, 181, 182.

pital at Rome on January 19, 1564, and signed by Coldwell, Bishop of St. Asaph, as well as other English refugees. The second document is a paper dated at Rome on May 3, 1564, and signed by Vincentius Parpaglia Abbas S. Solutoris Turine, which relates the message which the Pope gave to Sackville to relate to Elizabeth. Maitland interpreted this message to mean

> that Elizabeth was once more told that if she would enter the Catholic fold she might be as legitimate as the Pope could make her, and that there would be no trouble about the spoils of the monasteries. On the other hand, no hint is given of any approval of her prayer book or any compromise in matters of faith or worship.[55]

In summarizing the principal conclusions of this chapter, we note that Maitland suggested that Elizabeth's use of "etc." in her title was a mark of genius because it postponed a definite decision on the relationship of the sovereign to the Church of England. He gave Elizabeth the benefit of the doubt when he suggested that in critical times her conduct was governed by religious considerations rather than by a calculating nature. Maitland openly refuted the contention that Queen Elizabeth was forced to leave the Roman church because of harsh treatment at the hands of Pope Paul IV. An examination of the original parchment of the Act of Supremacy suggested to Maitland the nature of the struggle in both Commons and the House of Lords which resulted in modification of this bill before it was enacted into law.

J. B. Black agrees with Maitland that Elizabeth's use of "etc." was a shrewd maneuver. Neale concurs with the general

[55] *Ibid.*, 182, 183.

tenor of this conclusion. Hubert Hall disagreed with Maitland, while A. F. Pollard pointed out that Mary had used this expression earlier. Even Pollard, however, accepted Maitland's explanation of why Elizabeth resorted to this stratagem. Maitland is in the minority in his estimate of the strength of Elizabeth's religious convictions. Strachey, Read, and Black take a contrary position. Historians had long held that Elizabeth was not forced to leave the Roman church, but Maitland was the first to meet the issue directly and document his conclusion. His analysis of the document of the Act of Supremacy is certainly penetrating, as is attested by Neale in retracing Maitland's steps.

Maitland's account of the Elizabethan religious settlement indicates once again that he could not relate even a relatively well-known incident without finding some historical problems for his inquisitive mind to work on. He seemed to have an intuitive sense of knowing where and how to attack a given question. Maitland's general account is considered to be a thorough piece of work which passes carefully but judiciously through a field full of loaded issues and yet avoids offending any who could tolerate a dispassionate piece of work. His five articles encompassed by the general title "Elizabethan Gleanings" each developed a relatively minor facet of the story, and yet each has remained an enduring contribution.

AFTER HALF A CENTURY

THE HISTORY OF ENGLISH LAW encompasses the fields of both law and history. Maitland passed from the study and practice of law to exploring its history. Both of these disciplines are richer for his life of scholarly devotion and achievement. Although he had not deliberately planned his approach to what proved to be his consuming passion, he could hardly have pursued a more systematic course to prepare himself for the study of the history of English law, and he suggested that other less than successful barristers should turn to the history of English law.

It seems inevitable that the history of the past must be rewritten and reapplied to answer the questions and needs of each succeeding generation. Maitland was not content to accept the questions and answers which had been given concerning English law by such accepted authorities as Coke and Blackstone or, for that matter, even Stubbs. His probing curiosity and quest for truth compelled him to challenge their assumptions and question their conclusions. This led him to the task of editing rolls and Year Books as well as examining documents whose contents were usually considered to have been explored definitively. He was never content to accept the conclusions of other scholars if he could examine the original documents for himself.

Maitland's quizzical nature together with his scholarly discipline resulted in the turning of many a forgotten manuscript and the resurrection of many a historical problem that was considered to have been solved. He was always hopeful that his beating of the bushes might scare up a bird that was worthy of shot. In many cases his beating merely confirmed accepted conclusions and added new evidence to substantiate hypotheses already advanced. He had the ability to reglean an area and marshal his evidence in support of a conclusion in such a convincing manner that one must be bold indeed to reopen the subject. Maitland's refusal to accept any interpretation merely because it was hoary with age resulted in the stirring up of many a skeleton which had long rested in silence.

His boldness in challenging and disproving long-established historical tradition can be illustrated by his writings on Roman canon law in the Church of England. He contended that Roman canon law was accepted automatically by the English church until the time of the break with Rome under Henry VIII. The Anglican church and English historians in general had held that a canon law distinct from that of the Roman church had developed in England during the Middle Ages. The contention that the English church decided what part of the Roman canon law should be accepted or rejected as the canon law of England was denied by Maitland, who was able to show that it was the King, and not the English church, who forbade the enforcement of certain parts of the Roman canon law in England.

In the areas in which Maitland has been successfully challenged he was the victim of his strong bent toward law and the impact of law upon history. Although he readily proclaimed that much that we can learn of the social and economic life of the Middle Ages must be learned from legal documents, he himself was not particularly interested in these areas and hence failed to ask the questions which those who have followed in his steps have raised. In some areas, particularly in the Anglo-Saxon period and the origin of the borough, his conclusions must be modified because of an increased knowledge of the economic and social conditions of the times. Even here, however, Maitland indicated that there was a question in his own mind about his proficiency in these areas. He would have been the first to praise and congratulate those who through further research have modified and hence corrected his conclusions.

Maitland was probably the most stimulating scholar ever to turn his attention to the history of English law. It seems that most historians who have approached the subject have first looked to Maitland for inspiration. His mind was so keen that he turned up far more tracks than he ever could trail. Although this is to be expected of almost any scholar, Maitland had a unique ability to ask the right question or one which seldom ended in a fruitless pursuit.

He lent a quality of spirit to research and scholarship which has been a boon and an inspiration to young scholars ever since, for the young scholar can profit greatly by studying the life of Maitland to gain insight into technique and methodology as well as to glean the fruits of his scholarly research. Much of Maitland's writings were merely the skimmings of his research, which could with profit be refined and expounded and shared with a much wider audience than the group of scholars who might search them out in the form and the places in which he left them. I do not mean to imply that Maitland could not and did not express himself forcefully and coherently, but admittedly most of what he wrote was directed to his scholarly colleagues.

Wherever and whenever the history of English law is studied seriously, the name of Frederick William Maitland will be held in high esteem. His writings are now more than half a century old, but few of them are merely gathering dust on shelves. Wherever scholarship is appreciated, Maitland will be acclaimed.

THE F. W. MAITLAND
BIBLIOGRAPHY

THERE HAVE BEEN TWO NOTABLE EFFORTS to compile a bibliography of the writings of Maitland. Each has much to commend it, but each is beset with certain weaknesses. In the following bibliography, I have endeavored to utilize the strengths of each and to avoid the shortcomings.

A. L. Smith compiled a bibliography of Maitland's works soon after Maitland's death. This bibliography, together with two lectures, was published in 1908 *(Frederic William Maitland: Two Lectures and a Bibliography*. Cambridge, University Press). After checking Smith's work very carefully, I have come to the conclusion that it contains no mechanical errors. Its principal deficiency is in its omissions—it is incomplete.

A recent effort can be found in *The Maitland Reader* edited by V. T. H. Delany (New York, Oceana Publications, 1957). He acknowledges the aid of Mr. David L. Moore of the New York University Law Library in preparing his bibliography. Apparently one of Mr. Moore's signal contributions was the compiling of lists of the reviews of Maitland's lectures published in law journals in the United States and Canada. I am indebted to *The Maitland Reader* for these lists of reviews of

THE F. W. MAITLAND BIBLIOGRAPHY

Maitland's lectures which were published posthumously. I have adopted Mr. Delaney's divisions for the bibliography: Maitland's Works, Reviews of Maitland's Works, and Biographical Notices. Delany's bibliography contains a number of typographical errors, which, together with certain omissions, detract from its usefulness. A collation of these two bibliographies quickly suggests the need for a complete and accurate Maitland bibliography. I trust that the following pages will fill this lacuna.

MAITLAND'S WRITINGS

1875. "A Historical Sketch of Liberty and Equality." Fellowship dissertation. *Collected Papers,* I, 1–161.

1879. "The Law of Real Property," *Westminster Review.* *Collected Papers,* I, 162–201.

1880. "The Relation of Punishment to Temptation," *Mind,* pp. 259–64.

1881. "The Laws of Wales—The Kindred and the Blood Feud," *Law Magazine and Review,* Vol. VII, 344–67. *Collected Papers,* I, 202–29.

1882. "The Criminal Liability of the Hundred," *Law Magazine and Review,* Vol. VIII, 367–80. *Collected Papers,* I, 230–46.

1883. "Mr. Herbert Spencer's Theory of Society, I, II," *Mind,* pp. 354–71, 506–24. *Collected Papers,* I, 247–303.

"From the Old Law Courts to the New," *English Illustrated Magazine,* pp. 3–15.

"The Early History of Malice Aforethought," *Law Mag-*

azine and Review, IX, 406–426. *Collected Papers,* I, 304–28.

1884. *Pleas of the Crown for the County of Gloucester before the Abbot of Reading, 1221.* Edited by F. W. Maitland. London.

1885. *Justice and Police. The English Citizen.* London, Macmillan and Company.

"The Seisin of Chattels," *Law Quarterly Review,* Vol. I, 324–41. *Collected Papers,* I, 329–57.

1886. "The Mystery of Seisin," *Law Quarterly Review,* Vol. II, 481 ff., 496 ff. *Collected Papers,* I, 358–84.

"The Deacon and the Jewess; or, Apostasy at Common Law," *Law Quarterly Review,* Vol. II, 153–65. *Collected Papers,* I, 385–406.

"John le Breton." *Dictionary of National Biography,* II, 1183. Edited by Sir Leslie Stephen and Sir Sidney Lee. 22 vols. London, Oxford University Press. Reprinted in 1949–50.

1887. *Bracton's Note-Book. A Collection of cases decided in the king's court during the reign of Henry the Third.* Annotated by a lawyer of that time, seemingly by Henry of Bratton. Edited by F. W. Maitland. 3 vols. London, Clay.

1888. *Select Pleas of the Crown, Vol. I, 1200–1225.* Edited by F. W. Maitland. Selden Society, Vol. I. London, Bernard Quaritch, 1888. "Leet and Town" (Section II) in *Historical Essays,* 41–51.

"Why the History of English Law is Not Written," *Collected Papers,* I, 480–97.

"The Suitors of the County Court," *English Historical Review*, Vol. III, 417–21. *Collected Papers*, I, 458–66. (Review) *"Commons and Common Fields*. By T. E. Scrutton," *English Historical Review*, Vol. III, 568–70.

"The Beatitude of Seisin, I, II," *Law Quarterly Review*, Vol. IV, 24–39, 286–99. *Collected Papers*, I, 407–57.

"The Shallows and Silences of Real Life," *The Reflector*, Vol. I, 113–17. *Collected Papers*, I, 467–79.

1889. "The Surnames of English Villages," *Archaeology Review*, pp. 233–40. *Collected Papers*, II, 84–95.

"Possession for a Year and a Day," *Law Quarterly Review*, Vol. V, 253–64. *Collected Papers*, II, 61–80.

Select Pleas in Manorial and Other Seignorial Courts, Vol. I, Reigns of Henry III and Edward I. Selden Society, Vol. II. Edited by F. W. Maitland. London, Bernard Quaritch.

"The Introduction of English Law into Ireland," *English Historical Review*, Vol. IV, 516–17. *Collected Papers*, II, 81–83.

"The Materials for English Legal History, I, II," *Political Science Quarterly*, Vol. IV, 496–518, 628–47. *Collected Papers*, II, 1–60.

"Fleta," *Dictionary of National Biography*, VII, 290. Reprinted, London, 1949–50.

1890. (Letter) "Domesday Measures of Land," *Archaeology Review*, pp. 381–82.

"Ranulf de Glanvill," *Dictionary of National Biography*, VII, 1292–94. Reprinted, London, 1949–50.

"Northumbrian Tenures," *English Historical Review,* Vol. V, 625–32. *Collected Papers,* II, 96–109.

(Review) *"Year Books of Edward III. Years 14 and 15.* Edited and translated by Luke Owen Pike. 1889," *English Historical Review,* Vol. V, 592–93.

"The History of the Register of Original Writs," *Harvard Law Review,* Vol. IV, 97–115, 167–79, 212–25. *Collected Papers,* II, 110–73.

"Remainders after Conditional Fees," *Law Quarterly Review,* Vol. VI, 22–26. *Collected Papers,* II, 174–81.

"Slander in the Middle Ages," *The Green Bag,* Vol. II, 4–7.

1891. *The Court Baron . . . together with Select Pleas from the Bishop of Ely's Court of Littleport.* Edited by F. W. Maitland and William Paley Baildon. Selden Society, Vol. IV. London, Bernard Quaritch.

"The 'Praerogative regis'," *English Historical Review,* Vol. VI, 367–72. *Collected Papers,* II, 182–89.

(Review) "A Descriptive Catalogue of Ancient Deeds in the Public Record Office, Vol. I. 1890," *English Historical Review,* Vol. VI, 562–63.

"A Conveyancer in the Thirteenth Century," *Law Quarterly Review,* Vol. VII, 63–69. *Collected Papers,* II, 190–201.

Three Rolls of the King's Court, 1194–1195. Edited by F. W. Maitland. Pipe Roll Society, Vol. XIV.

"A New Point on Villein Tenure," *Law Quarterly Review,* Vol. VII, 174–75. *Collected Papers,* II, 202–204.

"Frankalmoign in the Twelfth and Thirteenth Centuries," *Law Quarterly Review*, Vol. VII, 354–63. *Collected Papers*, II, 205–22.

(Review) *"Walter of Henley's Husbandry. Transcripts, &c.* By E. Lamond. 1890," *Economic Journal*, pp. 225–26.

(Review) *"The Gild Merchant.* By Charles Gross. 2 vols. 1890," *Economic Journal*, pp. 220–24. *Collected Papers*, II, 223–31.

1892. "Henry II and the Criminous Clerks," *English Historical Review*, Vol. VII, 224–34. *Collected Papers*, II, 232–50.

"The 'Quadripartitus,'" *Law Quarterly Review*, Vol. VIII, 73–75.

(Review) *"Étude sur la Condition des Populations Rurales du Roussillon au Moyen Age.* Par J. A. Brutails. 1891. *Les Masuirs.* Par P. Errera. 1891," *English Historical Review*, Vol. VII, 748–54.

"Court Rolls, Manorial Accounts and Extents," *Palgrave's Dictionary of Political Economy*, I, 447–48. Edited by Henry Higgs. 3 vols. London, Macmillan and Company, Ltd., 1925–26.

"Glanvill Revised," *Harvard Law Review*, Vol. VI, 1–20. *Collected Papers*, II, 266–89.

1893. *Records of the Parliament Holden at Westminster, on the 28th Day of February, 1305.* Edited by F. W. Maitland. Rolls Series, Vol. LXXXXVIII. London, Eyre and Son. The "Introduction to the *Memoranda de Parlia-*

mento, 1305," is included in *Selected Essays,* 1–72, and in *Historical Essays,* 52–96.

(Review) *"Studien zur Rechtsgeschichte des Gottesfrieden und Landfrieden.* Vol. I. Von L. Huberti, 1892," *English Historical Review,* Vol. VIII, 328–31. *Collected Papers,* II, 290–97.

"History from the Charter Roll," *English Historical Review,* Vol. VIII, 726–33. *Collected Papers,* II, 298–312.

(Review) *"Superstition and Force.* H. C. Lea. 4th ed., 1892. *Ordines judiciorum dei nel missale gallicano del xii secolo della cattedrale di Palermo.* Di F. G. La Mantia. 1892," *English Historical Review,* Vol. VIII. 755–56.

(Review) *"The Early History and Influence of the Office of Coroner.* By Charles Gross. 1892." *English Historical Review,* Vol. VIII, 758–60.

"Taltarum's Case," *Law Quarterly Review,* Vol. IX, 1–2. *Collected Papers,* II, 310–12.

"The Survival of Archaic Communities: I, The Malmesbury Case. II, The Aston Case," *Law Quarterly Review,* Vol. IX, 36–50, 211–26. *Collected Papers,* II, 313–65.

"John Gorham Maitland," *Dictionary of National Biography,* XII, 811. Reprinted, London, 1949–50.

"Old English Law," *Social England,* I, 164–73. Edited by Henry Duff Traill. 6 vols. London, Cassell and Company, Ltd., 1893–97.

"English Law under Norman Rule," *Social England,* I, 274–85.

"Trial by Jury," *Social England,* I, 285–99.

"Growth of Jurisprudence," *Social England,* I, 408–11.

1894. (Review) *"Consiliatio Cnuti.* Von F. Liebermann. 1893,"*English Historical Review,* Vol. IX, 137–38.

"The History of a Cambridgeshire Manor," *English Historical Review,* Vol. IX, 417–39. *Collected Papers,* II, 366–402; *Historical Essays,* 16–40.

(Review) *"Forschungen Zur Geschichte des deutschen und französischen Rechtes.* Von H. Brunner. 1894," *English Historical Review,* Vol. IX, 593–94.

(Review) *"The Mark in Europe and America.* By E. A. Bryan," *English Historical Review,* Vol. IX, 598–99.

(Review) *"Die Anfange des Lehngerichtsbarkeit in England.* Von F. Zinkeisen," *English Historical Review,* Vol. IX, 600.

(Review) *"Uber die Leges Anglorum saeculo XII ineunte Londoniis collectae.* Von F. Liebermann, 1894,"*English Historical Review,* Vol. IX, 741–42.

"Legal Reform under Edward I," *Social England,* II, 32–38. Edited by Henry Duff Traill. 6 vols. London, Cassell and Company, Ltd., 1893–97.

"Outlines of English Legal History, 560–1600," *Social England,* II, 476–89. Edited by H. D. Traill. 6 vols. London, Cassell and Company, Ltd., 1893–97. Includes "English Law, 1307–1600," *Historical Essays,* 122–34.

"The Origin of Uses and Trusts," *Harvard Law Review,* Vol. VIII, 127–37. *Collected Papers,* II, 403–16.

1895. *The History of English Law before the Time of Edward*

I. By Sir Frederick Pollock and F. W. Maitland. 2 vols. Cambridge, University Press.

The Mirror of Justices. Edited by William Joseph Whittaker, with an introduction by F. W. Maitland. Selden Society Vol. VII.

Selected Passages from the Works of Bracton and Azo. Edited by F. W. Maitland. Selden Society Vol. VIII.

"The Murder of Henry Clement," *English Historical Review,* Vol. X, 294–97. *Collected Papers,* III, 11–16.

(Review) "*Two Chartularies of the Priory of St. Peter at Bath.* Edited by W. Hunt. The Somerset Record Society. 1893," *English Historical Review,* Vol. X, 558–60. *Collected Papers,* III, 17–20.

(Review) "*The History of Marriage, Jewish and Christian, in Relation to Divorce and Certain Forbidden Degrees.* By H. M. Lucock. 1894," *English Historical Review,* Vol. X, 755–59. *Collected Papers,* III, 21–30.

(Review) "*Cornelii Taciti de Germania.* Edited by H. Furneau," *English Historical Review,* Vol. X, 779–81.

(Review) "*The Tribal System in Wales.* By Frederick Seebohm. 1895," *Economic Journal,* pp. 589–94. *Collected Papers,* III, 1–10.

1896. "The Origin of the Borough," *English Historical Review,* Vol. XI, 13–19. *Collected Papers,* III, 31–42.

"A Song on the Death of Simon de Montfort," *English Historical Review,* Vol. XI, 314–18. *Collected Papers,* III, 43–49.

"Canon Law in England," *English Historical Review,* Vol. XI, 446–78, 641–72.

(Review) *"The Crawford Collection of Early Charters and Documents*. Edited by A. S. Napier and W. H. Stevenson. 1895," *English Historical Review*, Vol. XI, 557–58.

"Wyclif on English and Roman Law," *Law Quarterly Review*, Vol. XII, 76–78. *Collected Papers*, III, 50–53.

" 'Execrabilis' in the Common Pleas," *Law Quarterly Review*, Vol. XII, 174–80. *Collected Papers*, III, 54–64.

1897. *Domesday Book and Beyond*. Cambridge, University Press.

(Review) *"Developments of Trial by Jury*. By J. B. Thayer. Part I. 1896," *English Historical Review*, Vol. XII, 147–48.

(Review) *"Year Books of 16 Edward III*. Part I. Edited and translated by Luke Owen Pike. 1896," *English Historical Review*, Vol. XII, 350–51.

(Review) *"Le Livre de l'Abbé Guillaume de Ryckel*. Par H. Pirenne," *English Historical Review*, Vol. XII, 552.

"Canon Law in England," *English Historical Review*, Vol. XII, 625–58.

"A Plea for the Codification of English Law, IX," *New Century Review*, Vol. II, 52–53.

"Magistri Vacarii summa de matrimonio," *Law Quarterly Review*, Vol. XIII, 133–43, 270–87. *Collected Papers*, III, 87–105.

"Canon Law," *Encyclopaedia of the Laws of England*, II, 354–59.

"Burgage Tenure," *Encyclopaedia of the Laws of England*, II, 302–303.

"Court Baron and Court Leet," *Encyclopaedia of the Laws of England*, IV, 3–7.

1898. *The History of English Law before the Time of Edward I*. By Sir Frederick Pollock and F. W. Maitland. 2 vols. 2nd ed. Cambridge, University Press.

Township and Borough: The Ford Lectures. Cambridge, University Press. *Historical Essays*, 3–15.

Magistri Vacarii summa de matrimonio. Edited by F. W. Maitland. Reprinted from *Law Quarterly Review*, Vol. XIII (1897), 133–43. *See above*.

Roman Canon Law in the Church of England, a collection of six essays which had been published earlier, principally in the *English Historical Review*. London.

(Review) *"L'opere d'Irnerio*. Par Dr. E. Besta. 2 vols. 1896," *English Historical Review*, Vol. XIII, 143–44.

(Review) *"The Records of the Honourable Society of Lincoln's Inn. The Black Books*. Vol. I. 1422–1586. 1897," *English Historical Review*, Vol. XIII, 576–78.

(Review) *"Yorkshire Inquisitions*. Vol. II. Edited by W. Brown. Yorkshire Archaeological Society Record Series, Vol. 23. 1898," *English Historical Review*, Vol. XIII, 775–76.

(Review) *"Les collections canoniques attribuées à Yves de Chartres*. Par M. P. Fournier. 1897," *English Historical Review*, Vol. XIII, 815–16.

"A Prologue to a History of English Law," *Law Quarterly Review*, Vol. XIV, 13–33.

1899. (Review) *"Étude sur la propriété foncière dans les villes du moyen age.* Par G. de Marez. 1898," *English Historical Review,* Vol. XIV, 137–41.

"An Unpublished 'revocatio' of Henry II," *English Historical Review,* Vol. XIV, 735–37. *Collected Papers,* III, 115–18.

"Canon MacColl's New Convocation," *Fortnightly Review,* pp. 926–35. *Collected Papers,* III, 119–36. *Historical Essays,* 247–58.

"Round's 'Commune of London,' " *The Athenaeum,* October 21, 1899. *Historical Essays,* 259–65.

(Circa) "The Body Politic," *Collected Papers,* III, 285–303; *Selected Essays,* 240–56.

1900. *Political Theories of the Middle Ages.* By Otto Friedrich von Gierke. Translated, with an introduction, by F. W. Maitland. Cambridge, University Press.

"Elizabethan Gleanings, I–IV," *English Historical Review,* Vol. XV, 120–24, 324–30, 530–32, 757–60. *Collected Papers,* III, 157–209; *Historical Essays,* 211–46.

(Review) *"Documents relatifs à l'histoire de l'industrie et du commerce en France.* Par G. Fagniez. 1898," *English Historical Review,* Vol. XV, 142–43.

(Review) *"The Records of the Honourable Society of Lincoln's Inn. The Black Books, Vol. II, 1568–1600.* 1898," *English Historical Review,* Vol. XV, 170–71. *Collected Papers,* III, 76–86.

"The Corporation Sole," *Law Quarterly Review,* Vol. XVI, 335–54. *Collected Papers,* III, 210–43; *Selected Essays,* 73–103.

1901. *The Charters of the Borough of Cambridge.* Edited by F. W. Maitland and Mary Bateson. Cambridge, University Press.

Essays on the Teaching of History. By F. W. Maitland, H. M. Gwatkin, R. L. Poole, W. E. Heitland, W. Cunningham, J. R. Tanner, W. H. Woodward, C. H. Marten and W. H. Ashley. Cambridge, University Press.

English Law and the Renaissance. The Rede Lecture. Cambridge, University Press. *Historical Essays,* 135–51.

"Canon Law in England. A Reply to Dr. MacColl," *English Historical Review,* Vol. XVI, 35–45. *Collected Papers,* III, 137–56.

"William Stubbs, Bishop of Oxford," *English Historical Review,* Vol. XVI, 417–26. *Collected Papers,* III, 495–511. *Historical Essays,* 266–76.

"The Crown as a Corporation," *Law Quarterly Review,* Vol. XVII, 131–46. *Collected Papers,* III, 244–70; *Selected Essays,* 104–27.

"A Survey of the Century: II: Law," *Twentieth Century,* pp. 164–69. *Collected Papers,* III, 432–39.

1902. (Review) *"La lettre de foire à Ypres au XIII siècle.* Par G. de Marez. 1901," *English Historical Review,* Vol. XVII, 555–56.

(Review) *"The Pension Book of Gray's Inn, 1569–1660.* By R. J. Fletcher. 1901," *English Historical Review,* Vol. XVII, 613–14.

"Lord Acton," *Cambridge Review,* October 16, 1902. *Collected Papers,* III, 512–21.

"History of English Law," *Encyclopaedia Britannica*, XXVIII, 246–53. *Historical Essays,* 97–121.

(Circa) "The Unincorporated Body," *Collected Papers,* III, 271–84. *Selected Essays,* 128–40.

1903. *Year Books of Edward II, Vol. I, 1307–1309.* Edited by F. W. Maitland. Selden Society, Vol. XVII. London, Bernard Quaritch.

(Review) *"The Oldest Code of Laws in the World.* Translated by C. H. W. Johns. 1903," *Journal of the Society of Comparative Legislation,* N. S., Vol. XL, 10–12.

"Anglican Settlement and the Scottish Reformation," *Cambridge Modern History,* II, 550–98. *Historical Essays,* 152–210.

"Elizabethan Gleanings. V.," *English Historical Review,* Vol. XVIII, 517–32. *Collected Papers,* III, 157–209.

(Review) *"Court Rolls of the Manor of Ingoldsmells in the County of Lincoln.* Translated by W. O. Massingberd. 1902. Yorkshire Inquisitions, Vol. III, Yorkshire Archaeological Society Record Series, Vol. XXXI," *English Historical Review,* Vol. XVIII, 780–82.

1904. *"Trust und Korporation," Grunhut's Zeits.* f. das Priv. —U. Offentl.—Recht, Vol. XXXII. *Collected Papers,* III, 321–404; *Selected Essays,* 141–222.

Stephen (Sir L.) Hobbes. By John Morley. *English Men of Letters.* Seen through the press by F. W. Maitland. *Year Books of Edward II. 1308–1309, 1309–1310.* Selden Society, Vol. XIX. London, Bernard Quaritch.

1905. *Year Books of Edward II. 1309–1310.* Selden Society, Vol. XX. London, Bernard Quaritch.

"Moral Personality and Legal Personality" (Sidgwick Lecture, 1903). *Journal of the Society of Comparative Legislation,* N. S., No. 14, pp. 192–200. *Collected Papers,* III, 304–20; *Selected Essays,* 223–39.

"Sir Leslie Stephen," *Proceedings of the British Academy,* 1903–1904, pp. 316–20. *Collected Papers,* III, 522–30.

1906. "Henry Sidgwick," *Independent Review,* Vol. IX, 324–31. *Collected Papers,* III, 531–40.

"The Making of the German Civil Code," *Independent Review,* Vol. X, 211–21. *Collected Papers,* III, 474–88.

"Canon Law," *Encyclopaedia of the Laws of England* (2nd ed.), II, 541–46.

(Review) *"State Trials of the Reign of Edward I. 1289.* Edited by T. F. Tout and H. Johnstone. 1906," *English Historical Review,* Vol. XXI, 783–86.

De Republica Anglorum. By Sir T. Smith. Edited by L. Alston. With a preface by F. W. Maitland. Cambridge, University Press.

The Life and Letters of Leslie Stephen. London, Duckworth and Company.

"Miss Mary Bateson," *Athenaeum,* p. 736. *Collected Papers,* III, 541–43; *Historical Essays,* 277–78.

1907. *Year Books of Edward II, 1309–1311.* Edited by F. W. Maitland and G. J. Turner. Selden Society, Vol. XXIII. London, Bernard Quaritch.

The Constitutional History of England. Edited by H. A. L. Fisher. Cambridge, University Press.

1909. *Equity: Also the Forms of Action at Common Law.* Edited by A. H. Chaytor and W. J. Whittaker. Cambridge, University Press.

1910. *The Eyre of Kent.* Edited by F. W. Maitland, L. W. V. Harcourt, and W. C. Bolland. Selden Society, Vol. XXIV. London, Bernard Quaritch.

1911. *The Collected Papers of Frederic W. Maitland.* Edited by H. A. L. Fisher. 3 vols. Cambridge, University Press.

1912. *The Eyre of Kent,* Vol. II. Edited by F. W. Maitland, L. W. V. Harcourt, and W. C. Bolland. Selden Society, Vol. XXVII. London, Bernard Quaritch.

1913. *The Eyre of Kent,* Vol. III. Edited by F. W. Maitland, L. W. V. Harcourt, and W. C. Bolland. Selden Society, Vol. XXIX. London, Bernard Quaritch.

1915. *A Sketch of English Legal History.* With Francis C. Montague. Edited by J. F. Colby. New York, G. P. Putnam's Sons.

1936. *Equity: A Course of Lectures.* Edited by A. H. Chaytor and W. J. Whittaker. Revised by J. Brunyate. Cambridge, University Press.

Maitland: Selected Essays. Edited by H. D. Hazeltine, G. Lapsley, and P. H. Winfield. Cambridge, University Press.

1939. "The Anglo-French Law Language," *The Cambridge History of English Literature,* I, 455–60. Edited by A.

W. Ward and A. R. Waller. 15 vols. New York, The Macmillan Company.

1942. "From the Old Law Courts to the New," *Cambridge Law Journal,* Vol. VIII, 2 ff. Reprinted from *English Illustrated Magazine,* 1883.

1957. *Frederic William Maitland Reader.* Edited by Vincent Thomas Hyginns Delany. New York, Oceana Publications.

Selected Historical Essays of F. W. Maitland. Edited by Helen M. Cam. Cambridge, University Press. Published in association with the Selden Society.

1958. *Political Theories of the Middle Ages.* By Otto Friedrich von Gierke. Translated, with an introduction, by F. W. Maitland. Reprinted, Boston, Beacon Press.

1960. *Frederic William Maitland: Historian.* Selections from his writings, edited, with an introduction, by Robert Livingston Schuyler. Berkeley and Los Angeles, University of California Press.

REVIEWS OF MAITLAND'S WORKS

Pleas of the Crown for the County of Gloucester.
1884. By F. P[ollock]. *Law Quarterly Review,* Vol. I, 117–19.

Justice and Police.
1885. *Law Quarterly Review,* Vol. I, 385.
Saturday Review, Vol. LX, 199–200.
Athenaeum, June, 1885, p. 757.
1886. *Notes and Queries,* 7th Series, Vol. I, 500.

Select Pleas of the Crown. Vol. I.

1888. By J. H. Round. *English Historical Review,* Vol. III, 788–89.
By L. O. Pike. *Law Quarterly Review,* Vol. IV, 462–64.

Bracton's Note-Book.

1888. *Athenaeum,* pp. 10–11.
1889. By C. Elton. *English Historical Review,* Vol. IV, 154–61.

"Why the History of English Law Is Not Written."

1889. *Law Quarterly Review,* Vol. V, 93–94.

Select Pleas in Manorial Courts.

1890. By J. H. Round. *English Historical Review,* Vol. V, 586–87.

Records of the Parliament Holden at Westminster, 1305.

1894. *Notes and Queries.* 8th series, Vol. VI, 240.
Athenaeum, pp. 273–74.

Pollock and Maitland's *History of English Law before Edward I.*

1895. By W. J. Ashley. *Economic Journal,* pp. 581–85.
By Sir E. Fry. *English Historical Review,* Vol. X, 760–68.
Athenaeum, pp. 635–36.
By T. C. Williams. *Juridical Review,* July.
By M. M. Bigelow. *American Historical Review,* Vol. I, 112–20.
By J. J. Halsey. *Dial,* Vol. XX, 44.
Spectator, pp. 534–36.
By G. B. A[dams]. *Yale Review,* November.

The Mirror of Justices.

1895. By F. P[ollock]. *Law Quarterly Review,* Vol. XI, 534–36.

Pollock and Maitland's *History of English Law before Edward I.*

1896. *Edinburgh Review*, 428–48.
    By H. Brunner. *Political Science Quarterly*, 534–44.
    Oxford Magazine, Vol. XV, 300–301.
    Notes and Queries, 8th series, Vol. XI, 259.

Domesday Book and Beyond.

1897. By J. Tait. *English Historical Review*, Vol. XII, 768–77.
    Academy, pp. 396–97.
    By C. M. Andrews. *American Historical Review*, Vol. III, 130–33.

Township and Borough.

1898. *Law Magazine and Review*, 274–75.
    Guardian, pp. 1088–99.
    By C. Gross. *American Historical Review*, Vol. IV, 143–45.
    "Cambridge as She Was." Signed "F." *Cambridge Review*, Vol. XIX, 390–91.
1899. By J. Tait. *English Historical Review*, Vol. IV, 344–46.
    Notes and Queries, 9th series, Vol. III, 259.

Roman Canon Law in the Church of England.

1898. *Law Quarterly Review*, p. 205.
    By F. Y. P[owell]. *Law Quarterly Review*, pp. 311–14.
    By C. M. Andrews. *Political Science Quarterly*, pp. 707–11.
1899. *American Catholic Quarterly*, April.
    By H. Rashdall. *English Historical Review*, Vol. XIII, 144–47.
    Law Magazine and Review, pp. 243–44.
    Cambridge Review, Vol. XX, 278.
1900. By J. Hopwood. *Dublin Review*, pp. 67–90.
    By M. Smith. *Political Science Quarterly*, pp. 158–62.

Political Theories of the Middle Ages, by Otto Friedrich von Gierke. Translated, with an introduction, by F. W. Maitland.

1901. By W. G. P. Smith. *English Historical Review,* Vol. XVI, 370–72.
By F. P[ollock]. *Law Quarterly Review,* Vol. XVII, 95–96.
Cambridge Review, Vol. XXII, 317.
Athenaeum, 133–34.
Oxford Magazine, Vol. XX, 138.

English Law and the Renaissance.

1902. By H. Goudy. *English Historical Review,* Vol. XVII, 358–61.
Law Quarterly Review, Vol. XVIII, 98.

Pollock and Maitland's *History of English Law before Edward I.*

1902. By M. S[mith]. *Political Science Quarterly,* 718–19.

Year Books of Edward II, 1307–1309.

1904. By F. P[ollock]. *Law Quarterly Review,* Vol. XX, 94.

The Life and Letters of Leslie Stephen.

1906. By Sir F. Pollock. *Independent Review,* Vol. XI, 349–56.

Year Books of Edward II. 1308–1309.

1906. *Juridical Review,* pp. 301–303.

The Constitutional History of England.

1909. By H. P. MacMillan. *Juridical Review,* Vol. XXI, 277.
By C. M. Andrews. *American Political Science Review,* Vol. III, 616.

Equity: Also the Forms of Action at Common Law.
1909. *Juridical Review,* Vol. XXI, 277.
    Irish Law Times and Solicitors' Journal, Vol. XLIII, 271.
    Scottish Law Review, Vol. XXV, 244.
    Illinois Law Review, Vol. V, 55.
    Law Magazine and Review, Vol. XXXV, 356.
    Columbia Law Review, Vol. X, 681.
    The Green Bag, Vol. XXIV, 397.

The Collected Papers of Frederick William Maitland.
Edited by H. A. L. Fisher.
1911. By P. Vinogradoff. *The Nation.*
    By T. C. W[illiams]. *Law Quarterly Review,* Vol. XXVII, 474.
    Harvard Law Review, Vol. XXV, 574.
    By J. H. Wigmore. *Illinois Law Review,* Vol. VI, 418.
    Canadian Law Journal, Vol. XLVIII, 6.
    Canadian Law Times, Vol. XXXII, 390.

A Sketch of English Legal History. With Francis C. Montague. Edited by J. F. Colby.
1915. *Illinois Law Review,* Vol. X, 380.
    Case and Comment, Vol. XXII, 615.
    Kentucky Law Journal, Vol. IV, 12.
1916. *Michigan Law Review,* Vol. XIV, 437.
    University of Pennsylvania Law Review, Vol. LXIV, 414.
    By Joseph Warren. *Harvard Law Review,* Vol. XXIX, 351.
    Yale Law Journal, Vol. XXV, 251.
    Columbia Law Review, Vol. XVI, 363.
    California Law Review, Vol. IV, 511.
    By H. W. Edgerton, *Cornell Law Quarterly,* Vol. II, 66.
1923. *Justice of the Peace,* LXXXVII, 754.
1924. *Law Quarterly Review,* Vol. XL, 252.
1928. By P. L. Sayre. *Independent Law Journal,* Vol. III, 339.

Equity: A Course of Lectures. Edited by A. H. Chaytor and W. J. Whittaker. Revised by J. Brunyate.

1937. *Scottish Law Review,* Vol. LVII, 12.
  Law Journal, Vol. LXXXIII, 16.
  By S. P. Simpson. *Harvard Law Review,* Vol. L, 710.
  By W. S. Holdsworth. *Yale Law Journal,* Vol. XLVI, 801.
  By C. A. Wright. *Canadian Bar Review,* Vol. XV, 386.
  By A. W. Scott. *Brooklyn Law Review,* Vol. VI, 499.
  University of Pennsylvania Law Review, Vol. LXXXV, 866.
  By S. E. Thorne. *American Bar Association Journal,* Vol. XXIII, 983.
  Georgetown Law Journal, Vol. XXVI, 181.
  The Irish Jurist, Vol. III, 55.
  Journal of the Society of Public Teachers of Law, 54.
  Kentucky Law Journal, Vol. XXVI, 77.
  By J. H. C. Morris. *Law Quarterly Review,* Vol. LIII, 429.
  Modern Law Review, Vol. I, 86.
1938. *University of Toronto Law Journal,* Vol. II, 478.

The Forms of Action at Common Law. Edited by A. H. Chaytor and W. J. Whittaker.

1937. By S. P. Simpson. *Harvard Law Review,* Vol. L, 710.
  The Irish Jurist, Vol. III, 43.
  Journal of the Society of Public Teachers of Law, 54.
1938. *University of Toronto Law Journal,* Vol. II, 478.

Selected Essays. Edited by H. D. Hazeltine, G. Lapsley, and P. H. Winfield.

1937. By S. E. Thorne. *American Bar Association Journal,* Vol. XXIII, 983.
  Georgetown Law Journal, Vol. XXVI, 183.
  Law Quarterly Review, Vol. LIII, 574.
  By S. P. Simpson. *Harvard Law Review,* Vol. L, 710.

FREDERICK WILLIAM MAITLAND

Modern Law Review, Vol. I, 93.

University of Toronto Law Journal, Vol. II, 478.

1938. *The Irish Jurist,* Vol. IV, 7.

By R. L. Severns. *Chicago-Kent Review,* Vol. XVI, 209.

BIOGRAPHICAL NOTICES, ETC.

1893. "A reference to a member of the Selden Society undertaking to bear the expenses of the publication of Maitland's edition of *Bracton and Azo. Academy,* p. 172.

1904. "Professor Maitland: Biographical Notice and Portrait," *Journal of the Society of Comparative Legislation,* N. S., No. 12, p. 9.

1906. "On the Death of Professor Maitland," *The Times,* December 22, 1906, p. 6.

"The Late Professor Maitland," *Journal of the Society of Comparative Legislation,* N. S., No. 16, p. 581.

"F. W. Maitland, 1850–1906," by Sir Frederick Pollock, *Proceedings of the British Academy,* Vol. II (1905–1906), 455–59.

1907. "On the Death of Frederick William Maitland," by A. J. Butler, *Athenaeum,* pp. 15–16.

"Maitland: A Word More," signed A. J. B[alfour], *Athenaeum,* p. 47.

"On the Death of Professor Maitland," *Law Quarterly Review,* Vol. XXIII, 11.

"Frederic William Maitland," signed A. L. S[mith]. *Oxford Magazine,* January 23, 1907, pp. 150–51.

"Professor Maitland," *Cambridge Review,* January 17, 1907, p. 160.

"In Memoriam. F. W. Maitland," by O. W. Holmes, *Law Quarterly Review,* Vol. XXIII, 136–50.

"Frederick William Maitland," by Thomas Seccombe, *The Bookman,* February, 1907, pp. 216–21.

"Frederick William Maitland," by Sir Frederick Pollock, *Law Quarterly Review,* Vol. XXIII, pp. 401–19.

"Foreign Impressions of F. W. Maitland," *Law Quarterly Review,* Vol. XXIII, 137–50.

"American Impressions of F. W. Maitland," *Political Science Quarterly,* June, 1907, pp. 287–90.

"Proceedings at the Maitland Memorial Meeting," *Cambridge University Reporter,* July 22, 1907, pp. 1301 ff.

Memoir by Benjamin Fossett Lock in *Year Books of Edward II,* 3 and 4. Selden Society, Vol. XXII. Edited by Maitland, but published after his death.

"Maitland," by Benjamin Fossett Lock, *Solicitor's Journal,* January 5, 1907.

"Maitland," by Sir Paul Vinogradoff, *English Historical Review,* Vol. XXII, 280–89.

"Maitland," by Munro Smith, *Political Science Quarterly* (New York), pp. 282 ff.

"Maitland," by D. P. Heatley, *Juridical Review,* April, 1907.

"Maitland," by G. T. Lapsley, *The Green Bag*, Vol. XIX.

1908. *Frederic William Maitland: Two Lectures and a Bibliography*, by A. L. Smith. Oxford, University Press.

1910. *Frederic William Maitland*, by Herbert Albert Laurens Fisher. Cambridge, University Press.

"Maitland," by John Horace Round, *Peerage and Pedigree*, Vol. I, 145–47.

1911. "Maitland," by T. F. Tout, *Scottish Historical Review*, pp. 73–75.

"Life of F. W. Maitland," by B. F. Lock, in *Dictionary of National Biography*, 1901–1911, pp. 552–55.

1912. "The Evolution of Professor Maitland," *Canadian Law Times*, Vol. XXXII, 390 ff.

1913. "Frederic William Maitland, 1850–1906. In Memoriam," by William Searle Holdsworth, *Law Magazine and Review*, Vol. XXXIX, 8 ff.

1916. "Frederic William Maitland," by Charles H. Haskins, *Proceedings of the American Academy of Arts and Sciences*, Vol. LI (No. 13), 504–505.

1923. "F. W. Maitland," by W. W. Buckland, *Cambridge Law Journal*, Vol. I, 131–43.

1924. "Gossip about Legal History: Unpublished Letters of Maitland and Ames," introduction by H. D. Hazeltine, *Cambridge Law Journal*, Vol. II, 1–18.

1927. "Maitland and the Story of English History," by W. S. Holdsworth, *Ia. S. B. A.*, pp. 202 ff.

1928. *Vinogradoff's Collected Papers.* Edited by H. A. L. Fisher. 2 vols. Oxford, University Press, 1928. I, 253–64; 265–71.

1937. "Maitland as a Sociologist," by Ernest Barker. *Sociological Review,* Vol. XXIX, 121–35.

1950. "F. W. Maitland: 1850–1950," by R. J. White, *The Cambridge Journal,* pp. 131–43.

1951. "A Memoir of F. W. Maitland," by Mrs. Reynell, *Cambridge Law Journal,* Vol. XI, 67–73.

"F. W. Maitland," by Theodore Frank Thomas Plucknett, *New York University Law Review,* Vol. XXVI, 1 ff.

"Maitland's View of Law and History," by Theodore Frank Thomas Plucknett, *Law Quarterly Review,* Vol. LXVII, 179–94.

"Maitland and the Corporate Revolution," by M. T. Rooney, *New York University Law Review,* Vol. XXVI, 24 ff.

1952. *Fredegond and Gerald Shove.* By Fredegond Shove. (With a preface by Ermengard Maitland.) Privately printed.

"The Historical Spirit Incarnate: Frederic William Maitland," by Robert Livingston Schuyler, *American Historical Review,* Vol. LVII, 303–22.

1953. *Frederic William Maitland, 1850–1906: A Memorial Address.* By Henry Arthur Hollond. The Selden Society Annual Lecture. London, Bernard Quaritch.

1955. *Modern Historians and the Study of History.* By Frederick Maurice Powicke. London, Odhams Press, Ltd.

1956. *Law and History in the Nineteenth Century.* By C. H. S. Fifoot. Selden Society Lecture.

1957. *F. W. Maitland: A Child's-Eye View.* By Ermengard Maitland. Selden Society.

GENERAL BIBLIOGRAPHY

Adams, George Burton. "Anglo-Saxon Feudalism," *American Historical Review,* Vol. VII (1901–1902), 11–35.

———. *Constitutional History of England.* Revised by Robert L. Schuyler. New York, Henry Holt and Company, 1934.

———. *Council and Courts in Anglo-Norman England.* New Haven, Yale University Press, 1926.

———. "The Origin of the Common Law," *Yale Law Journal,* Vol. XXX (1924), 115–28; chapter V in *Council and Courts in Anglo-Norman England.*

———. "The Origin of the English Constitution," *American Historical Review,* Vol. XIII (1908–1909), 229–45; 713–30.

———. *The Origin of the English Constitution.* 2nd ed. New Haven, Yale University Press, 1920.

Ault, Warren O. "The Maitland-Bigelow Letters," *Boston University Law Review,* Vol. XXXVII (1957), 285–326.

———. "Some Early Village By-Laws," *English Historical Review,* Vol. XLV (1930), 208–31.

———. "Village By-Laws by Common Consent," *Speculum,* Vol. XXIX (1954), 375–94.

Baldwin, James Fosdick. *The King's Council in England During the Middle Ages.* Oxford, Clarendon Press, 1913.

Ballard, Adolphus. *British Borough Charters, 1024–1216.* Cambridge, University Press, 1913.

———. *The Domesday Boroughs.* Oxford, Clarendon Press, 1904.

———. *Domesday Inquest.* London: Methuen and Company, 1906.

Bateson, Mary (ed). *Borough Customs.* 2 vols. Selden Society, Vols. XVIII, XXI. London, Bernard Quaritch, 1904, 1906.

———. "Review of *The Domesday Boroughs* by Adolphus Ballard, Oxford: at the Clarendon Press, 1904," *English Historical Review,* Vol. XX (1905), 143–51.

Bayne, C. G. "The First House of Commons of Queen Elizabeth," *English Historical Review,* Vol. XXIII (1908), 455–76, 643–82.

Bigelow, Melvin M. *Placita Anglo-Normanica: Law Cases from William I to Richard I.* Boston (printed in London), Little, Brown and Company, 1879.

Black, J. B. *The Reign of Elizabeth, 1558–1603.* Oxford, Clarendon Press, 1936.

Brooke, Z. N. "The Effects of Becket's Murder on Papal Authority in England," *Cambridge Historical Journal,* Vol. II (1927).

———. *The English Church and the Papacy.* Cambridge, University Press, 1931.

Cam, Helen M. "The Community of the Vill," *Medieval Studies Presented to Rose Graham,* 1–14. Edited by V. Ruffer and A. J. Taylor. Oxford, University Press, 1950.

———. "The Evolution of the Mediaeval English Franchise," *Speculum,* Vol. XXXII (1957), 427–42.

———. "Review of *The Medieval English Borough: Studies on Its Origin and Constitutional History.* By James Tait. Manchester: University Press, 1926," *English Historical Review,* Vol. LII (1937), 303–306.

———. "The 'Private' Hundred before the Norman Conquest," *Studies Presented to Sir Hilary Jenkinson,* 50–59. Oxford, University Press, 1957.

Cheney, C. R. "Legislation of the Medieval English Church," *English Historical Review,* Vol. L (1935), 193–224; 385–417.

Cheney, Mary. "The Compromise of Avranches of 1172 and the Spread of Canon Law in England," *English Historical Review,* Vol. LVI (1941), 177–97.

Clapham, J. H., and Eileen Power (eds.). *The Cambridge Economic History of Europe from the Decline of the Roman Empire.* Vol. I. Cambridge, University Press, 1941.

Collingwood, R. G., and J. N. L. Myres. *Roman Britain and the English Settlements.* 2nd ed. Oxford, Clarendon Press, 1945.

Croome, H. M., and R. J. Hammond. *An Economic History of Britain.* With a Foreword by Lord Beveridge. London, Christophers, 1948.

Cunningham, W. *The Growth of English Industry and Commerce During the Early and Middle Ages.* 3 vols. 5th ed. Cambridge, University Press, 1910.

Darlington, R. R. "Review of *From Domesday Book to Magna Carta, 1087–1216.* By A. L. Poole. Oxford: Clarendon Press, 1951," *English Historical Review,* Vol. LXVII (1952), 563–66.

Davis, E. Jeffries. "An Unpublished Manuscript of the Lords' Journal for April and May, 1559," *English Historical Review,* Vol. XXVIII (1913), 531–42.

Dodwell, Barbara. "East Anglian Commendation," *English Historical Review*, Vol. LXIII (1948), 289–306.

Donaldson, Gordon. "The Attitude of Whitgift and Bancroft to the Scottish Church," *Transactions of the Royal Historical Society*, Fourth Series, Vol. XXIV, 95–115. London, 1942.

Douglas, David C., and George W. Greenaway (eds.). *English Historical Documents, 1042–1189*. Vol. II of *English Historical Documents*, ed. by David C. Douglas. New York, Oxford University Press, 1953.

Edwards, J. G. "The Personnel of the Commons in Parliament under Edward I and Edward II," *Essays in Medieval History Presented to Thomas Frederick Tout*, 197–214. Edited by A. G. Little and F. M. Powicke. Manchester, published for the subscribers, 1925.

Flower, Cyril Thomas (ed.). *Curia Regis Rolls*, 1199–1230. Selden Society, Vol. LXII (1943). London, Bernard Quaritch, 1944.

Freeman, Edward A. *The Growth of the English Constitution*. London, Macmillan and Company, 1898.

Frere, W. H. *The English Church in the Reigns of Elizabeth and James I, 1558–1625*. Vol. V of *A History of the English Church*. Edited by W. R. W. Stephens and William Hunt. 8 vols. London, Macmillan and Company, Ltd., 1904.

Froude, James Anthony. *History of England from the Fall of Wolsey to the Death of Elizabeth*. 12 vols. New York, Charles Scribner and Company, 1870.

Galbraith, V. H. "The Making of Domesday Book," *English Historical Review*, Vol. LVII (1942), 161–77.

Gibbs, Marion, and Jane Lang. *Bishops and Reform, 1215–1272*. Oxford, Clarendon Press, 1934.

Gneist, Rudolf von. *The History of the English Constitution*.

Translated by Philip A. Ashworth. 2 vols., London, W. Cloves and Sons, 1886.

Gomme, Sir George Laurence. *The Village Community, with Special Reference to the Origin and Form of Its Survival in Britain.* New York, Charles Scribner's Sons, 1907.

Gooch, George Peabody. *History and Historians in the Nineteenth Century.* London and New York, Longmans, Green, 1913.

Gras, Norman Scott Brien. *The Economic and Social History of an English Village.* Cambridge, Mass., Harvard University Press, 1930.

Gray, Howard Levi. *English Field Systems.* Cambridge, Mass., Harvard University Press, 1915.

Gross, Charles. *Gild Merchant: A Contribution to British Municipal History.* 2 vols. Oxford, 1890.

Hale, Sir Mathew. *Jurisdiction of the Lords House: or Parliament Considered According to Its Ancient Records.* London, T. Cadell, and W. Davis, 1796.

Haskins, George L. *The Growth of English Representative Government.* Philadelphia, University of Pennsylvania Press, 1948.

————. "The Petitions of Representatives in the Parliaments of Edward I," *English Historical Review,* Vol. LIII (1938), 1–20.

Hazeltine, H. D. "Roman and Canon Law in the Middle Ages," *The Cambridge Medieval History,* V, 697–764. Planned by J. B. Bury; edited by H. M. Gwatkin and J. P. Whitney. 8 vols. New York, The Macmillan Company, 1936.

Holdsworth, William Searle. *A History of English Law.* 9 vols. 3rd ed. London, Methuen and Company, 1922–25.

Howlett, Richard. "Village Communities," *Palgrave's Dictionary of Political Economy,* III, 621–24. Edited by Henry Higgs. 3 vols. London, Macmillan and Company, Ltd., 1926.

Hoyt, Robert S. "Farm of the Manor and Community of the Vill in Domesday Book," *Speculum,* Vol. XXX (1955), 147–69.

———. "The Nature and Origins of the Ancient Demesne," *English Historical Review,* Vol. LXV (1950), 145–74.

———. "Recent Publications in the United States and Canada on the History of Representative Institutions before the French Revolution," *Speculum,* Vol. XXIX (1954), 356–77.

———. *The Royal Demesne in English Constitutional History: 1066–1272.* Ithaca, Cornell University Press, for the American Historical Association, 1950; London, Cumberlege, 1951.

Hurnard, Naomi D. "The Anglo-Norman Franchises," *English Historical Review,* Vol. LXIV (1949), 289–320, 433–460.

———. "The Jury of Presentment and the Assize of Clarendon," *English Historical Review,* Vol. LVI (1941), 374–410.

Innes, Arthur Donald. *England under the Tudors.* London, Methuen and Company, 1905; New York, Putnam, 1926.

Jenks, Edward. *Law and Politics in the Middle Ages.* New York, Henry Holt and Company, 1898.

Jolliffe, J. E. A. *The Constitutional History of Medieval England: From the English Settlement to 1484.* London, Adam and Charles Black, 1948.

———. "Some Factors in the Beginnings of Parliament," *Transactions of the Royal Historical Society,* Fourth Series, Vol. XXII, 101–39. London, 1940.

Kimball, Elizabeth G. "Tenure in Frank Almoign and Secular Services," *English Historical Review,* Xol. XLIII (1928), 341–53.

Lapsley, Gaillard. "Some Recent Advance in English Constitutional History (before 1485)," *The Cambridge Historical Journal,* Vol. V (1936), 119–61. Reprinted in *Crown, Community, and Parliament.* Oxford, 1951.

Lipson, E. *The Economic History of England,* Vol. I, *The Middle Ages.* 7th ed. London, Adam and Charles Black, 1937.

Little, A. G., and F. M. Powicke (eds.). *Essays in Medieval History Presented to Thomas Frederick Tout.* Manchester, published for the subscribers, 1925.

MacColl, Malcom. *The Reformation Settlement.* London, 1899; revised, 1901.

McIlwain, Charles Howard. *The High Court of Parliament; And Its Supremacy.* New Haven, Yale University Press, 1910.

McKechnie, William Sharp. *Magna Carta: A Commentary on the Great Charter of King John,* with an Historical introduction. Glasgow, J. Maclehose and Sons, 1905. 2nd ed., 1914.

McKisack, May. "Borough Representation in Richard II's Reign," *English Historical Review,* Vol. XXXIX (1924), 511–25.

———. *The Parliamentary Representation of the English Boroughs During the Middle Ages.* Oxford, 1932.

Morris, William Alfred. *The Constitutional History of England to 1216.* New York, The Macmillan Company, 1930.

Neale, John Ernest. *Elizabeth I and Her Parliaments, 1559–1581.* New York, Jonathan Cape, 1953.

———. "The Elizabethan Acts of Supremacy and Uniformity," *English Historical Review,* Vol. LXV (1950), 304–22.

———. *Queen Elizabeth I.* London, Jonathan Cape, 1954.

Neilson, Nellie. "The Early Pattern of the Common Law," *American Historical Review,* Vol. XLIX (1944), 199–212.

———. "England," *The Cambridge Economic History of Europe from the Decline of the Roman Empire,* I, 438–466. Edited by J. H. Clapham and Eileen Power. Cambridge, University Press, 1941.

Norgate, Kate. *England under the Angevin Kings.* 2 vols. London and New York, Macmillan and Company, 1887.

———. *The Minority of Henry III.* London, Macmillan and Company, Ltd., 1912.

Pasquet, D. *Essay on the Origins of the House of Commons.* Translated by R. G. D. Laffan, with notes by G. T. Lapsley. Cambridge, University Press, 1925.

Petit-Dutaillis, Charles Edmond. *Studies and Notes Supplementary to Stubbs' Constitutional History.* Translated by W. E. Jones. Manchester, University Press, 1908.

Pike, Luke Owen. "An Action at Law in the Reign of Edward III: The Report and the Record," *Harvard Law Review,* Vol. VII (1894), 266–80.

———. *The Constitutional History of the House of Lords.* London, Macmillan Company, 1894.

———. "The Manuscripts of the 'Year Books' and the Corresponding Records," *The Green Bag: An Entertaining Magazine For Lawyers,* Vol. XII (1900), 533–42.

———. (trans. and ed.). *Year Books of Edward III.* 15 vols. London, Longman and Company, 1883–1911.

Plucknett, Theodore Frank Thomas. *A Concise History of the Common Law.* Rochester, New York, The Lawyers Co-operative Publishing Company, 1929.

———. *Legislation of Edward I: The Ford Lectures Delivered in the University of Oxford in Hilary Term 1947.* Oxford, Clarendon Press, 1949.

———. "Parliament," *The English Government At Work, 1327–1336,* I, 82–128. Edited by J. F. Willard, W. A. Morris, J. R. Strayer, and W. H. Dunham, Jr., 3 vols. Cambridge, Mass., The Medieval Academy of America, 1940–50.

———. (Review) *"Select Cases in the Court of King's Bench Under Edward I.* Vol. I. Edited by George O. Sayles, Selden Society, Vol. LV.; London: Bernard Quaritch, 1936," *English Historical Review,* Vol. LII (1937), 317–18.

Pollard, Albert Frederick. *The Evolution of Parliament.* London, Longmans, Green and Company, Ltd., 1926.

———. *The History of England from the Accession of Edward VI to the Death of Elizabeth, 1547–1603.* London, Longmans, Green and Company, 1910.

Poole, Austin Lane. *From Domesday Book to Magna Carta, 1087–1216.* Oxford, Clarendon Press, 1955.

———. "Letters from Maitland to R. L. Poole, Editor of the *English Historical Review,"* *Cambridge Historical Journal,* Vol. X (1952), 318 ff.

Poole, Reginald Lane. *The Exchequer in the Twelfth Century.* Oxford, Clarendon Press, 1912.

Post, Gaines. "The Two Laws and the Statute of York," *Speculum,* Vol. XXIX (1954), 417–32.

Powicke, Sir Frederick Maurice. *King Henry III and the Lord Edward.* Oxford, Clarendon Press, 1947.

———. *Modern Historians and the Study of History.* London, Odhams Press, Ltd., 1955.

———. (Review) *"Curia Regis Rolls of the Reign of Richard I and John.* Edited by C. T. Flower, 1922," *English Historical Review,* Vol. XXXIX (1924), 264–72.

———. (Review) *"Legislation of Edward I: The Ford Lectures Delivered in the University of Oxford in Hilary Term, 1947.* By T. F. T. Plucknett. Oxford: at the Clarendon Press, 1949," *English Historical Review,* Vol. LXVI (1951), 105–109.

————. *The Thirteenth Century, 1216–1307*. Oxford, Clarendon Press. 1953.

Ramsay, Sir James H. *Dawn of the Constitution, or the Reigns of Henry III and Edward I, 1216–1307*. New York, the Macmillan Company, 1908.

Rayner, Doris. "The Forms and Machinery of the 'Commune Petition' in the Fourteenth Century," *English Historical Review*, Vol. LVI (1941), 198–233, 549–70.

Read, Conyers. *Bibliography of British History, Tudor Period, 1485–1603*. Oxford, Clarendon Press, 1933.

————. *The Tudors: Personalities and Practical Politics in Sixteenth Century England*. New York, Henry Holt and Company, 1936.

Richardson, Henry Gerald. "The Origins of Parliament," *Transactions of the Royal Historical Society*, Fourth Series, Vol. XI. London, 1928.

Richardson, Henry Gerald, and George O. Sayles. "Early Records of the English Parliament," *Bulletin of the Institute of Historical Research*, Vol. V (1931), 129–54; Vol. VI (1932), 71–88, 129–55.

————. *The Irish Parliament in the Middle Ages*. Philadelphia, University of Pennsylvania Press, 1952.

————. "The King's Ministers in Parliament, 1277–1377," *English Historical Review*, Vol. XLVI (1931), 529–50; Vol. XLVII (1932), 194–203; 377–97.

————. "Parliaments of Edward III," *Bulletin of the Institute of Historical Research*, Vol. VIII (1934), 65–82; Vol. IX (1935), 1–18.

————. (eds.). *Rotuli Parliamentorum Anglie Hactenus Inediti MCLXXIX–MCCCLXXIII*. Camden third Series, Vol. LI. London, 1935.

Riess, Ludwig. "Der Ursprung des englischen Unterhauses," *Historische Zeitschrift,* Vol. LX (1888), 1–33.

———. *Geschichte des Wahlrects zum englischen Parlament im Mittelalter.* Leipzig, 1885.

———. *The History of the English Electoral Law in the Middle Ages.* Translated with additional notes, by Kathleen Louise Wood-Legh. Cambridge, University Press, 1940.

Round, John Horace. *Feudal England: Historical Studies on the 11th and 12th Centuries.* London, S. Sonneschein and Company, 1895.

———. *Geoffry de Manville: A Study of the Anarchy.* London, Longmans, Green and Company, 1892.

———. "The Origin of the House of Lords," reprinted in *Peerage and Pedigree,* I, 324–62. London, James Nisbet and Co., Ltd., 1910.

———. "The 'Tertius Denarius' of the Borough," *English Historical Review,* Vol. XXXIV (1919), 62–64.

Sayles, George O. (ed.). *Select Cases in the Court of King's Bench: Under Edward I.* 3 vols. Selden Society, Vols. 55, 57, and 58. London, Bernard Quaritch, 1936, 1938, and 1939.

Seebohm, Frederick. *The English Village Community.* Cambridge, University Press, 1926.

Soule, Charles C. "Year Book Bibliography," *Harvard Law Review,* Vol. XIV (1901), 557–87.

Stenton, Doris Mary. *English Society in the Early Middle Ages (1066–1307).* Vol. III of *The Pelican History of England.* 2nd ed. Baltimore, Penguin Books, Inc., 1952.

——— (ed.). *Rolls of the Justices in Eyre, Being the Rolls of Pleas and Assizes for Lincolnshire, 1218–1219, and Worcester-*

shire, 1221. Selden Society, Vol. LIII. London, Bernard Quaritch, 1934.

Stenton, Frank M. *Anglo-Saxon England.* 2nd ed. Oxford, Clarendon Press, 1955.

——. *The First Century of English Feudalism, 1066–1166.* Oxford, Clarendon Press, 1932.

Stephenson, Carl. "The Aids of the English Boroughs," *English Historical Review,* Vol. XXXIV (1919), 457–75.

——. "The Anglo-Saxon Borough," *English Historical Review,* Vol. XLV (1930), 177–207.

——. *Borough and Town.* Cambridge, Mass., The Medieval Academy of America, 1933.

——. "Commendation and Related Problems in Domesday," *English Historical Review,* Vol. LIX (1944), 289–310.

——. *Medieval Institutions: Selected Essays.* Edited by Bryce D. Lyon. Ithaca, Cornell University Press; London, 1954.

——. "The Problem of the Common Man in Early Medieval Europe," *American Historical Review,* Vol. LI (1946), 419–38.

——. "Taxation and Representation," *Haskins Anniversary Essays,* 291–312. Edited by C. H. Taylor. Boston, Houghton Mifflin, 1929.

——, and Frederick George Marcham (trans. and eds.). *Sources of English Constitutional History: A Selection of Documents from A.D. 600 to the Present.* New York and London, Harper and Brothers, 1937.

Strachey, Lytton. *Elizabeth and Essex.* New York, Harcourt, Brace and Company, 1928.

Stubbs, William. *The Constitutional History of England.* 3 vols. 5th ed. Oxford, Clarendon Press, 1891.

————. (ed.). *Gesta Regis Henrici Secundi Benedicti Abbatis.* 2 vols. London, Longmans, Green, Reader and Dyer, 1867.

————. *Historical Appendix to the Report of the Commissioners Appointed to Inquire into the Constitution and Working of the Ecclesiastical Courts.* London, Parliamentary Papers, XXIV (1883).

————. *Select Charters.* 9th ed. Revised by H. W. C. Davis. Oxford, Clarendon Press, 1913.

————. *Seventeen Lectures on the Study of Medieval and Modern History.* 3rd ed. Oxford, Clarendon Press, 1900.

Tait, James. "The Firma Burgi and the Commune in England, 1066–1191," *English Historical Review,* Vol. XLII (1927), 321–49.

————. "Liber Burgus," *Essays in Medieval History Presented to Thomas Frederick Tout,* 79–98. Edited by A. G. Little and F. M. Powicke. Manchester, published for the subscribers, 1925.

————. *The Medieval English Borough: Studies on Its Origin and Constitutional History.* Manchester, University Press, 1936.

————. "The Origin of Town Councils in England," *English Historical Review,* Vol. XLIV (1929), 177–202, 399.

Templeman, Geoffrey. "The History of Parliament to 1400 in the Light of Modern Research," *University of Birmingham Historical Journal,* Vol. I (1948), 202–31. Reprinted in *The Making of English History,* 109–27. Edited by R. L. Schuyler and H. Ausubel. New York, Dryden Press, 1952.

Usher, Abbott Payson. *An Introduction to the Industrial History of England.* Boston, Houghton Mifflin Company, 1920.

Vinogradoff, Sir Paul. *English Society in the Eleventh Century: Essays in English Mediaeval History.* Oxford, Clarendon Press, 1908.

————. *The Growth of the Manor.* 2nd ed. New York, Burt Franklin, 1951.

————. "The Roman Element in Bracton's Treatise," *Yale Law Journal,* Vol. XXXII (1926), 751–56.

————. *Roman Law in Medieval Europe.* London and New York, Harper and Brothers, 1909.

————. *Villainage in England: Essays in English Mediaeval History.* Oxford, University Press, 1892.

White, Albert Beebe. *The Making of the English Constitution, 449–1485.* 2nd ed. New York and London, G. P. Putnam's Sons, 1925.

Wilkinson, Bertie. *The Constitutional History of England, 1216–1399,* Vol. I, *Politics and the Constitution 1216–1307.* London and New York, Longmans, Green and Company, 1948.

Winfield, Percy Henry. *The Chief Sources of English Legal History.* Cambridge, Mass., Harvard University Press, 1925.

Woodbine, G. E. "The Roman Element in Bracton's *De Adquirendo rerum dominio,*" *Yale Law Journal,* Vol. XXXI (1925), 827–47.

INDEX

INDEX

INDEX

Pole, Reginald: 129
Pollard, A. F.: 151; interprets *in pleno parliamento*, 31, 45
Pollock, Sir Frederick: 17, 139; described Maitland, 3; authorship of *History of English Law*, 5; inspired Maitland, 9
Poole, Reginald L.: 20 f.
Port: 84
Powicke, F. M.: 58
Prayer book, second Edwardian: 157
Prisot, C. J.: 142
Privilegium fori: 78
Provinciale: 15, 67
Provisors: 76
Public Record Office: 7 f., 59; value of, 9

Quadra, Alvaro de: 158
Queen Elizabeth I: accession to the throne, 147; illegitimacy of, 148 n.; "etceterates" herself, 150 f.

Raleigh, William: 126
Ranke, L. von: 153
Report of the Ecclesiastical Courts Commission: 15, 62 f. 81
Richard of Ilchester: 49
Richardson and Sayles, on the nature of Parliament: 31 n., 43 n., 46
Riess, Ludwig: concept of Parliament, 27; challenged orthodox view of Parliament, 30 f.; on representation in Parliament of Edward I, 39 n.
Rochester, England: 89
Rogers, B. S., describes Maitland as a lawyer: 7, 13 n.
Rolls Series: 26
Roman Canon Law in the Church of England: 63, 81, 146
Roman law: 21; reception of, in the sixteenth century, 119; renaissance of, in the twelfth century, 124
Roman villa: 105, 115
Round, J. H.: 20 n., 22, 28
Runcorn, England: 86

Sackville, Thomas: 161
Sake, Maitland's explanation of: 6
Sayles, George O.: common law courts, 48; on origin of the court of common bench, 56 n.; on court of king's bench, 59
Schuyler, R. L.: 11, 15
Scotland, represented in the Parliament of 1305: 36
Scutage: 37
Seebohm, Frederick: 10; Romanist origin of the village, 100; challenged Germanists, 112 f.
Selden Society: 17 f., 21, 144 f., 134 f.
Select Pleas of the Crown: 39, 48
Sext: 64, 69
Smith, Thomas: 129
Stafford, England: 86
Statute of Carlisle, "*De Asportis religiosorum*": 37
Stenton, D. M.: views on *magnum concilium*, 35; on boroughs, 86; economic importance of towns, 92
Stephens, Leslie: 9
Stephenson, Carl: 89, 113 n.
Strachey, Lytton: 149, 152
Strathfield: 88
Stubbs, William: *xi* f., 21, 123 f.; distinct Anglican church and law, 15 n.; *Constitutional History*, 26; nature of Parliament, 27; on Parliament of Edward I, 28–30; on common law courts in the thirteenth century, 48; origin of court of king's bench, 51; on English canon law, 62, 81; Germanic origin of village, 100

Tait, James: 89; review of *Domesday Book and Beyond*, 22; borough courts, 93
Tallage: 37
Tamworth, England: 85
"Tenurial heterogeneity": 89, 91, 99
Terra Regis: 85
Teutonic law of England: 121

About 1750, John Baskerville, a wealthy manufacturer whose hobby was printing, set up his own type foundry and began experimenting with printing inks, paper, and the design of type. These experiments were to have a lasting influence on printing, although at one time they had the typographical world divided into rival camps. It seemed appropriate to use the type which had such an impact on the world of printing in a book about Frederick William Maitland, whose research has had an equally salutary effect on the writing of English history.

UNIVERSITY OF OKLAHOMA PRESS

NORMAN